I0794798

James Monroe

An Illustrated History

President James Monroe, by John Vanderlyn, 1822, on display in Old City Hall, New York.
ART COMMISSION OF THE CITY OF NEW YORK

James Monroe

An Illustrated History

BY DANIEL PRESTON

1908 2008
UNIVERSITY OF
MARY WASHINGTON
The Centennial Celebration

This book is published as part of the celebration of the centennial of the University of Mary Washington and the 250th anniversary of the birth of James Monroe, both of which occur in 2008.

Library of Congress Control Number 2008922172

ISBN 978-1-57510-138-5

Second Printing July 2016

Printed by Doosan Printing, Korea

Book Design & Typography by Arrow Graphics, Missoula, Montana
www.arrowgraphics.org

Published by
Pictorial Histories Publishing Company, Inc.
713 South Third Street West, Missoula, MT 59801
phone (406) 549-8488, fax (406) 728-9280
phpc@montana.com
website: pictorialhistoriespublishing.com

Table of Contents

ACKNOWLEDGMENTS

FIRST AND FOREMOST, I want to thank Heidi Stello and Laura Summers, my aides at the Papers of James Monroe, for their invaluable assistance in locating and organizing the images that appear in this book. Thanks to Meghan Budinger, the curator of the James Monroe Museum, for help in gaining access to the extensive collections at the Museum, and to Carolyn Holmes, director of Ash Lawn-Highland, for providing photographs of Monroe's home. Thanks also to the many curators and librarians who gave assistance by providing images. Thanks to John Pearce, director of the Monroe Museum, for helping to proofread the manuscript. Kitty Herrin of Arrow Graphics is responsible for the beautiful design of this book. Financial support for the project came from the University of Mary Washington Centennial Fund and the University of Mary Washington Foundation—thanks to Carter Hudgins, Bill Crawley, Jeff Rountree, and Rick Hurley. Support also came from Clan Munro, USA; thanks to them for their generous gift, and especially to Elizabeth Brand Monroe.

James Monroe

INTRODUCTION

JAMES MONROE'S REMARKABLE CAREER in public service began in early 1776 when, at age seventeen, he became an officer in the Continental Army and continued until December 1829, when he served as president of a convention in Richmond to revise the Virginia constitution. During his life Monroe took part in many of the great events in the history of the United States. Among these were the war for independence, the ratification of the Constitution, the election of Thomas Jefferson as president, the Louisiana Purchase, the War of 1812, the Missouri Compromise, the contentious election of 1824 and, of course, the pronouncement of the Monroe Doctrine.

Along the way, he held a vast array of public offices. He was an army officer during the Revolutionary War, was five times elected to the Virginia House of Delegates, was a member of the executive council of Virginia, represented his state in the Continental Congress, and was a delegate to the Virginia convention for the ratification of the U. S. Constitution. He sat in the U. S. Senate, was four times elected governor of Virginia, and held four diplomatic appointments: twice to France, once to Great Britain, and once to Spain. He served as both secretary of state and secretary of war during the Madison administration and served two terms as president of the United States. After leaving the presidency, he received an appointment to the county court (the governing body) of Loudoun County, Virginia and served as president of the Virginia constitutional convention of 1829.

Then there were the offers of appointment that he declined: state judge (twice), governor of Louisiana Territory (twice), delegate to the pan-American congress in Panama, a fifth nomination as governor, and candidate for vice president of the United States. He also lost several elections: once to the House of Delegates, once to the House of Representatives, and once for the presidency (in 1808).

At left: James Monroe, by Gilbert Stuart, ca. 1820.

METROPOLITAN MUSEUM OF ART, NEW YORK

CHRONOLOGY

28 April 1758
born Westmoreland County, Virginia, son of Spence and Elizabeth Monroe

30 June 1768
Elizabeth Kortright born (future Mrs. James Monroe)

June 1774
began studies at College of William and Mary

1774
Spence Monroe (father) died; inherited farm in Westmoreland County

February 1776
commissioned lieutenant in 3rd Virginia Infantry

16 September 1776
at Battle of Harlem Heights

28 October 1776
at Battle of White Plains

26 December 1776
wounded at Battle of Trenton

July 1777
promoted to captain

11 August 1777
began serving as aide-de-camp to General Stirling

11 September 1777
at Battle of Brandywine

4 October 1777
at Battle of Germantown

20 November 1777
promoted to major

James Monroe, by Rembrandt Peale, ca. 1825. James Monroe Museum and Memorial Library, Fredericksburg, VA

January–June 1778
at Valley Forge

28 June 1778
at Battle of Monmouth

20 December 1778
resigned from the Continental Army

15 August–15 December 1779
lieutenant-colonel in Virginia State Line assigned to Williamsburg

January 1780
began to study law with Thomas Jefferson

June–August 1780
with army in North Carolina as observer for Governor Jefferson

4 April 1782
elected to Virginia House of Delegates from King George County

June 1782
admitted to bar

7 June 1782
appointed to Council of State of Virginia

6 June 1783
elected to Continental Congress

23 December 1783
George Washington resigned as commander-in-chief of the Continental Army

14 January 1784
Congress ratified Treaty of Paris

1 March 1784
Virginia cession of western lands

July–October 1784
tour of Great Lakes and Canada

January 1785
Congress moved to New York

25 August–14 November 1785
trip to Kentucky

16 February 1786
married Elizabeth Kortright in New York

April 1786
lost election to Virginia House of Delegates

May 1786
proposed treaty with Spain rejected

13 October 1786
term in Congress ended

October 1786
established residence in Fredericksburg, VA; opened law office

December 1786
Eliza Monroe (daughter) born

April 1787
elected to Virginia House of Delegates from Spotsylvania County

2–27 June 1788
member Virginia constitutional ratifying convention; voted against ratification

October 1788
purchased farm in Albemarle County, VA; became resident of Albemarle County

2 February 1789
James Madison defeated Monroe in election to House of Representatives

9 November 1790
elected to U.S. Senate

1793
purchased another farm in Albemarle County (later named Highland)

28 May 1794
appointed minister to France

30 December 1796
mission to France ended

August 1797
returned to Charlottesville; began construction of house at Highland; returned to law practice

May 1799
James Spence Monroe (son) born

James Monroe, by Chester Harding, 1829. National Portrait Gallery, Washington, DC

23 November 1799
established residence at Highland

17 December 1799
began first term as governor of Virginia

30 August 1800
Gabriel's conspiracy exposed

28 September 1800
James Spence Monroe died

10 October 1800
Gabriel executed

4 March 1801
Jefferson inaugurated as president

April 1802
Maria Hester Monroe (daughter) born

September 1802
Elizabeth Monroe Buckner (sister) died

9 December 1802
term as governor expired

12 January 1803
appointed minister extraordinary to France

2 March 1803
appointed minister extraordinary to Spain

18 April 1803
appointed minister to Great Britain

30 April 1803
Louisiana Purchase treaty signed

1 January–26 May 1805
in Madrid for treaty negotiations

31 December 1806
signed treaty with Great Britain; not accepted by President Jefferson

November 1807
mission to Great Britain ended

21 January 1808
nominated for president by dissident Republicans in Virginia

July-August 1808
trip to Kentucky

28 September 1808
Eliza Monroe married George Hay

1808
acquired Oak Hill in Loudoun County, VA

April 1810
elected to Virginia House of Delegates from Albemarle County

May 1810
reconciliation with Madison

18 January 1811
began fourth term as governor of Virginia

2 April 1811
appointed secretary of state

18 June 1812
war declared on Great Britain

19 Dec. 1812–5 Feb. 1813
acting secretary of war

24 August 1814
British captured Washington

27 August 1814
appointed secretary of war; served concurrently as secretary of state

24 December 1814
Treaty of Ghent signed

1 January 1815
Battle of New Orleans

15 March 1815
resigned as secretary of war

October 1816
appointed to board of visitors for Central College (University of Virginia)

4 March 1817
inaugurated as president

20 April 1817
Rush-Bagot Treaty signed

June–September 1817
tour of northern states

6 October 1817
presided at laying of cornerstone of University of Virginia

April–May 1818
Jackson's invasion of Florida

May–June 1818
tour of Chesapeake Bay area

20 October 1818
US-Canadian border treaty

25 February 1819
Adams-Onis Treaty

April–July 1819
tour of southern states

James Monroe, by Charles Willson Peale, 1818. New York State Office of Parks, Recreation, and Historic Preservation, Waterford, NY

1819
began construction of new house at Oak Hill

3 March 1820
Missouri Compromise

9 March 1820
Maria Hester Monroe married Samuel Gouverneur

5 March 1821
inaugurated for second term as president

8 March 1822
recommended recognition of South American republics

2 December 1823
delivered annual message containing Monroe Doctrine

6 August 1824
Joseph J. Monroe(brother) died

4 March 1825
John Quincy Adams inaugurated

ca. 25 March 1825
retired to Oak Hill in Loudoun County

4 July 1826
Jefferson died

1 August 1826
appointed to board of visitors of University of Virginia

24 Oct 1826
declined appointment as delegate to convention of American nations in Panama

2 December 1826
Andrew Monroe (brother) died

January 1827
declined to be candidate for election as governor of Virginia

December 1827
declined to be candidate for election as vice president

July 1828
sold Highland

5 October–12 December 1829
president of Virginia constitutional convention

21 September 1830
George Hay (son-in-law) died

23 September 1830
Elizabeth Kortright Monroe died

October 1830
moved to New York City

14 May 1831
resigned from board of visitors of University of Virginia

4 July 1831
died in New York

BIRTH AND YOUTH

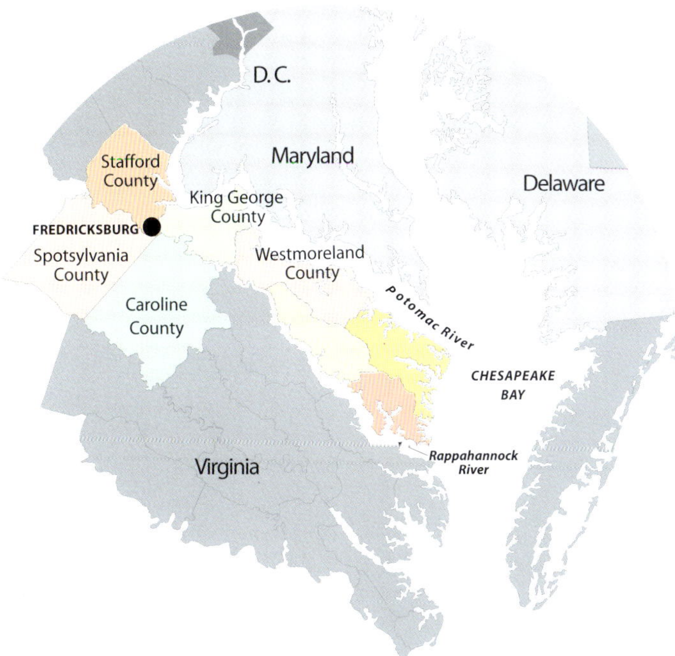

Monroe was born in Westmoreland County, Virginia in 1758. He made his home in Westmoreland, in adjoining King George County, and in nearby Fredericksburg until 1788. MAP BY ARROW GRAPHICS

JAMES MONROE was born in Westmoreland County, Virginia, on 28 April 1758, the son of Spence and Elizabeth Jones Monroe. The Monroes resided on a 350-acre farm on Monroe's Creek, several miles from the Potomac River (near present-day Colonial Beach). Andrew Monroe, the founder of the line in Virginia, emigrated to the colony from Scotland in 1650; James was of the fourth generation born in Virginia.

Little is known of Monroe's parents. Spence Monroe was a carpenter as well as a farmer. It is not known when his mother died, but perhaps it was in 1772 at the birth of her last child. Monroe barely mentioned them in his autobiography, saying only that his father "was a very worthy and respectable citizen possessed of good landed and other property." His mother, he wrote, "was a very amiable and respectable woman, possess-

Monroe's ancestors immigrated to Virginia from northern Scotland in 1650. Foulis Castle, near Inverness, is the present-day seat of Clan Munro.

HECTOR MUNRO, FOULIS CASTLE

"Sir Hector Monro has invited me and my family to Scotland to see him. He thinks he owns the farm my ancestors left."

—MONROE TO JOSEPH JONES, 28 JANUARY 1805.

ing the best domestic qualities, a good wife and good parent." When Spence Monroe died in 1774 (leaving the farm to James, his oldest son), Joseph Jones, the brother of Elizabeth Jones Monroe, became the guardian of the orphaned children.

Monroe had four siblings: an older sister named Elizabeth and three younger brothers: Spence, Andrew, and Joseph. Elizabeth married Richard Buckner, a planter who lived near Fredericksburg, and seems to have been close to James. Spence, who was a year younger than James, died in his youth, perhaps sometime around 1776. Andrew and Joseph spent their adult years living as dependents of their older brother. Andrew resided on a farm owned by James and passed largely unnoticed through life. Joseph's improvident living kept him constantly in debt, which James usually paid.

Monroe attended school at Campbelltown Academy, which was located near his home. This was one of the best schools in the colony, and boys came from other parts of Virginia to attend. One of these was John Marshall, the future chief justice of the United States, whose time at the academy overlapped briefly with that of Monroe. It is not known when Monroe began attending Campbelltown, but he left it in 1774 to become a student at the College of William and Mary in Williamsburg, the colonial capital.

The Monroe house in Westmoreland County was a small, two-story frame structure typical of middle-class farm houses in colonial Virginia. The engraving at left was published in 1845, when the house was in a dilapidated state.

Robert Sears, *Pictorial History of the American Revolution*

The footprint of the house, below, is based upon archaeological excavations at the site in 1976.

Virginia Department of Historic Resources

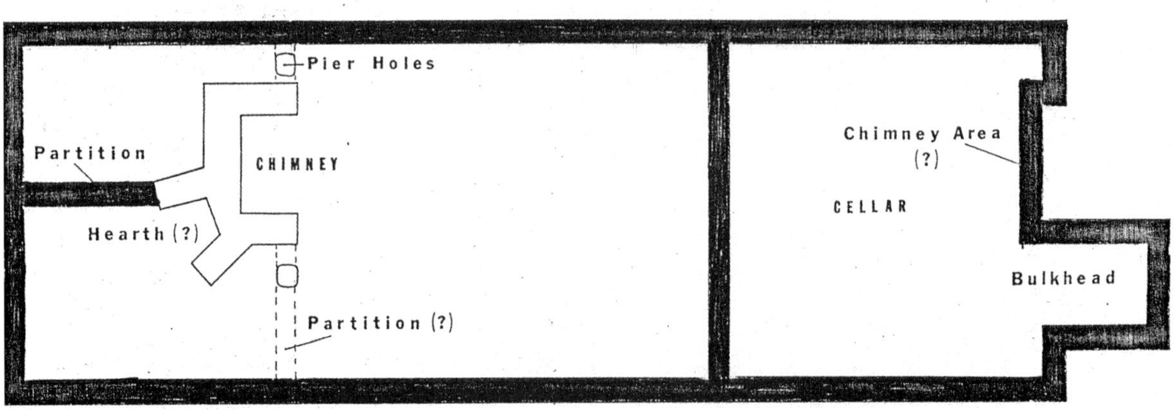

The Monroe birth site is now a county park. A state highway sign and a small obelisk mark the site.

PHOTOGRAPHS BY DANIEL PRESTON

Andrew Monroe
JAMES MONROE MUSEUM

SIBLINGS

James Monroe was the second of five siblings. His older sister, Elizabeth, married William Buckner and resided on a farm near Fredericksburg. Spence, the brother after James, died before 1776.

The two youngest brothers were completely lacking in ambition and depended on James for financial support. Andrew (above) spent most of his adult years living on a farm owned by James. "[Andrew] is an honest good hearted man, advancing in years, and in a great measure helpless," James wrote in 1814; "He don't appear to me to have any fixed plan and I presumes expects aid from me."

Joseph Jones Monroe (below), James' youngest brother, was trained as attorney but never attained a successful career. James tried to help Joseph establish himself—he paid for him to attend school in Scotland and taught him law—but to no avail. It appears that Joseph had a fondness for drinking and gambling, and relied on James to pay his debts.

Joseph Monroe
JAMES MONROE MUSEUM

THE FAMILY TREE OF JAMES MONROE

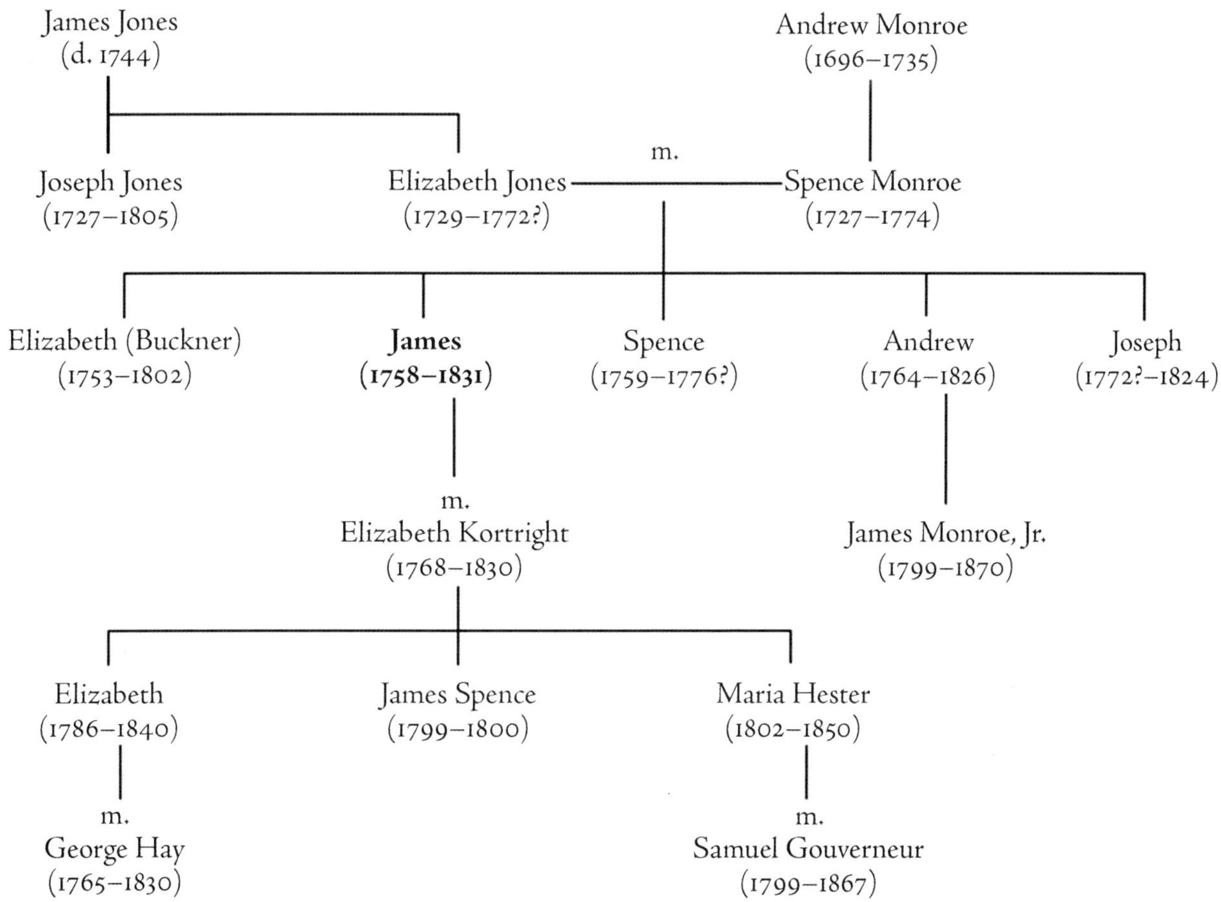

James Monroe

WILLIAMSBURG

JAMES MONROE became a student at the College of William and Mary in June 1774. He was sixteen years old, which was the normal age for entering the college. The course of study lasted two years, but Monroe's term was disrupted by the outbreak of the revolution, and he left after eighteen months. Monroe recalled later in life that while his previous education in the classics had been thorough, his knowledge of mathematics and other subjects was inadequate and that he had to work hard to master them.

Many of the students at William and Mary became leaders in Virginia, and Monroe had contact with many of them during the revolution and in later years in government. Three of these students became prominent among Monroe's future friends and associates: John Marshall, former fellow student at Campelltown Academy and the future chief justice of the United States; John Francis Mercer, whose family lived in the same area as the Monroes on the northern neck of Virginia and who became one of Monroe's closest friends while they served together in the Revolutionary War and in the Continental Congress; and William Short, another close friend and political associate who, for a while, owned a farm adjoining Monroe's in Albemarle County.

Being in Williamsburg, the most important and most cosmopolitian town in Virginia, was a great education for all the boys who came to the college from farms in the distant part of the colony. But it was especially so for Monroe and others who were there in 1774 and 1775 at the time of the agitation leading up to the revolution. Being in Williamsburg placed Monroe at the center of resistance to British imperial policy. The debates in the assembly, the presence of revolutionary leaders such as Patrick Henry, and the mustering of the revolutionary militia had a profound effect on Monroe and the many other students who became ardent supporters of the revolution.

Indeed, Monroe's active participation in the revolution began while he was still a student. Lord Dunmore, the last colonial governor of Virginia, amassed a large collection of arms at his residence in Williamsburg and displayed them in the foyer and in other rooms as symbols of the power of Great Britain. When Dunmore fled Williamsburg in June 1775, a party of students, including Monroe, raided the governor's house, seized these weapons, and delivered them to the revolutionary militia.

The College of William and Mary
Virginia Historical Society, Richmond

"Soon after I got there, a vacation took place, which lasted two months. I had been examined in Latin and Greek and found well qualified to enter the philosophical school. In that I was put to the study of mathematics, Euclid etc., and composing declamation, for which I was altogether unqualified, being only sixteen years of age. I made therefore a ridiculous figure. The vacation taking place, I applied the whole time to close study, so that when the lectures resumed, I had made such good use of my time, that I obtained the approbation and praise of the professors"

—Monroe to James Monroe Jr., 24 December 1813

A view of Williamsburg, painted by Thomas Millington in 1836, showing the College of William and Mary in the distance. Swem Library, College of William and Mary

Lord Dunmore, the last colonial governor of Virginia, sought to convey the power of Great Britain by displaying an extensive collection of arms in his residence in Williamsburg. When Dunmore fled the capital in June 1775, a party of students from the college—including James Monroe—raided the Governor's House, seized the arms, and delivered them to the revolutionary militia.

Colonial Williamsburg Foundation

FRIENDS

Monroe made several life-long friends at William and Mary. One was William Short who, like Monroe was a young protégé of Thomas Jefferson. Short served as U. S. minister to Spain in the 1790s at the time when Monroe was minister to France, and for a while owned a farm in Albemarle County, Virginia that adjoined Monroe's. (Painting by Rembrandt Peale, courtesy the Muscarelle Museum of Art, The College of William and Mary.)

Monroe had first met future chief justice John Marshall when both had attended Campbellton Academy in Westmoreland County. There was a rupture in their friendship when they took opposite sides in the bitter political battles of the 1790s, but they later reconciled and remained friends. (Portrait by Charles St. Memin, courtesy of the Library of Virginia, Richmond.)

John Francis Mercer was perhaps Monroe's closest friend during his early adulthood. They served together during the Revolutionary War and in the Continental Congress. Mercer later moved to Maryland and became governor of that state. (Painting courtesy of Maryland State Archives, Annapolis).

Joseph Jones, Monroe's maternal uncle, was a prominent Virginia jurist and political figure. He became Monroe's guardian in 1774 when Monroe's father died. Jones remained a trusted adviser and political patron until his death in 1805. He was in Williamsburg as a member of the Virginia convention while Monroe was a student at William and Mary.

Joseph Jones

James Monroe Museum

About Jones, Monroe said: "Few men possessed in a higher degree the confidence and esteem of his fellow citizens, or merited more, for soundness of intellect, perfect integrity, and devotion to his country."

—James Monroe, *Autobiography*

William Short

John Marshall

John Francis Mercer

James Monroe

THE AMERICAN REVOLUTION

"No approbation can be more dear to me than that of those with whom I have had the honour to share the common toils and perils of the war for our Independence. We were embarked in the same sacred cause of liberty, and we have lived to enjoy the reward of our common labours. . . . May your children never forget the sacred duties devolved on them to preserve the inheritance so gallantly acquired by their fathers. May they cultivate the same manly patriotism, the same disinterested friendship and the same political integrity, which has distinguished you, and thus unite in perpetuating the social concord and public virtue on which the future prosperity of our country must essentially depend."

—James Monroe to the Massachusetts Society of the Cincinnati, 4 July 1817

Above: Sword carried by Monroe during the Revolutionary War.

James Monroe Museum

Left: Monroe was severely wounded at Trenton while leading a charge against Hessians who were trying to set up an artillery position. This engraving (made from the painting by John Trumbull) shows a wounded Monroe on the ground to the left of General Washington.

Library of Congress, Prints and Photographs Division

JAMES MONROE left the College of William and Mary in February 1776 and became a lieutenant in the Third Virginia Infantry, which was being organized at Fredericksburg. The regiment was commanded by Colonel Hugh Mercer, a friend of his uncle. The regiment left Virginia in August and joined General Washington's army at New York on 12 September. Four days later Monroe saw combat for the first time in the battle at Harlem Heights.

General George Washington, by Charles Willson Peale. U. S. SENATE

"I saw him in my earliest youth, in the retreat through Jersey, at the head of a small band, or rather, in its rear, for he was always near the enemy, and his countenance and manner made an impression on me which time can never efface. . . . A deportment so firm, so dignified, so exalted, but yet so modest and composed, I have never seen in any other person."

—MONROE TO CONGRESS, 4 MAY 1822

Monroe accompanied the remnants of Washington's army as it retreated south to Pennsylvania. When Washington decided to attack Trenton, Monroe crossed the Delaware River the night before the battle with the advance guard sent ahead to secure the roads. Monroe was seriously wounded during the attack on Trenton by a gunshot wound to the shoulder. A doctor accompanying the advance guard tended his wound and probably saved his life. Washington awarded Monroe's gallantry by promoting him to captain. As was common practice, Monroe was sent home to Virginia to serve on recruiting duty while recovering from his wound.

Monroe returned to the army in August 1777. He was promoted to major and assigned to the staff of Major General William Alexander, Lord Stirling. He participated in the battles at Brandywine and Germantown, and spent the winter of 1777–1778 with the army at Valley Forge. The following summer he fought at the battle of Monmouth.

Monroe chafed at his staff duties and longed to return to a field command. There was a surplus of officers serving with the army, however, and no positions opened for him. He resigned from the Continental Army at the end of 1778 and returned home. There he was made a lieutenant colonel in the Virginia service and authorized to raise a regiment for the defense of the state. He was at Williamsburg from August 1779 to March 1780 trying to raise his regiment; he was unable to do so, however, since most eligible men were already in service. Monroe retained his rank as lieutenant colonel, and took to the field with the militia on several occasions, but did not have active command of a regiment of his own.

While at Williamsburg Monroe made the acquaintance of Governor Thomas Jefferson. Monroe contemplated returning to the College of William and Mary to study law with George Wythe, the most renowned legal scholar in the state. But when Jefferson and the state government moved from Williamsburg to Richmond in April 1780 Monroe went with them and began to study law under Jefferson's direction. During the summer of 1780 he was with the Continental army in North Carolina as an observer, sending reports back to Governor Jefferson on the British advance.

When this duty ended, Monroe went home to his farm to concentrate on the study of law. He joined the army at Yorktown in October 1781, but determined that his services were not needed and returned home. James Monroe's military career had ended.

Colonel Hugh Mercer was the commander of Monroe's regiment, the Third Virginia Infantry. Mercer was later promoted to brigadier general and died at the battle at Princeton, New Jersey in 1777. His statue, sculpted by Edward Valentine, stands in his home town of Fredericksburg, Virginia.

PHOTOGRAPH BY KAREN PEARLMAN

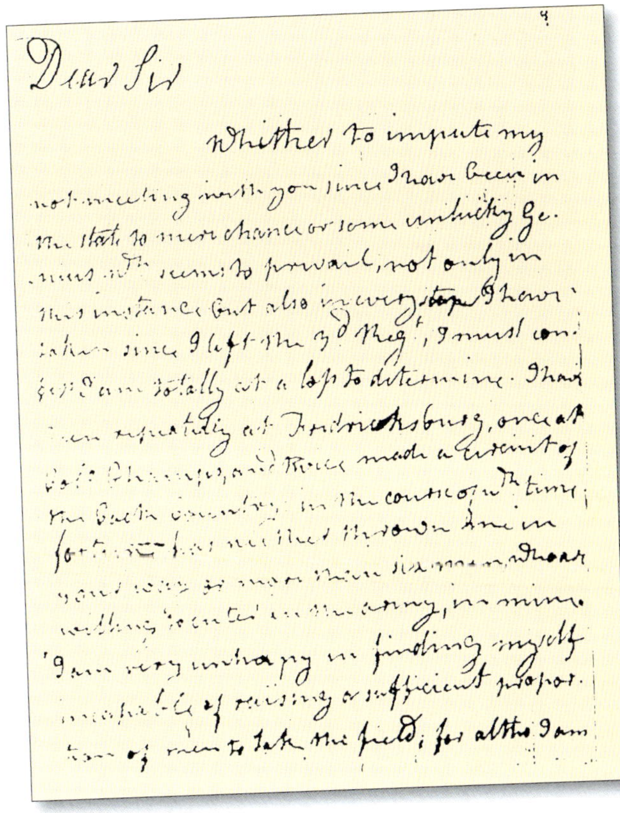

Dear Sir

Whither to impute my not meeting with you since I have been in the State to mere chance or some unlucky genius which seems to prevail, not only in this instance but also in every step I have taken since I left the 3d Reg^t, I must confess I am totally at a loss to determine. I have been repeatedly at Fredericksburg, once at [illegible] and thence made a circuit of the back country in the course of which time [illegible] I am very unhappy in finding myself incapable of raising a sufficient proportion of men to take the field; for altho I am

This letter, dated July 3, 1777 and addressed to Captain John Thornton, is the earliest known letter written by Monroe. It describes the difficulty of recruiting soldiers for the Continental Army.

VIRGINIA STATE ARCHIVES, RICHMOND: REJECTED CLAIMS: JOHN THORNTON

At about the time Monroe returned to the army, the Marquis de Lafayette joined Washington's forces with the rank of major general. Although there was a great difference in their rank Monroe and Lafayette were close in age (Lafayette was a year older), and the two became friends.

PORTRAIT BY CHARLES WILLSON PEALE,
INDEPENDENCE NATIONAL HISTORICAL PARK, PHILADELPHIA

The signing of the Declaration of Independence. John Trumbull, Yale University Art Museum

"The day on which the American Congress declared the thirteen British Colonies free and independent States was a very important day to mankind. If we critically examine the events of modern times or look back into the records of past ages we shall find nothing like it in the annals of nations. It was important as a measure of policy adopted with a view to secure to the good people of those States the great objects of the controversy. It was important as it dismembered the British empire and erected an independent power in the western hemisphere that was likely soon to be felt in all the great concerns of the eastern. But it was much more important as it introduced a system of government founded on the equal rights and sovereignty of the people under forms more perfect than any that were ever known before." —James Monroe, undated

Emanuel Luetze's famous painting of Washington crossing the Delaware depicts Lieutenant Monroe standing behind Washington holding the flag. Monroe actually crossed the river the night before as part of the advance guard sent to secure the roads into Trenton.

Metropolitan Museum of Art

"Three companies of that Regiment, Thorntons in which Mr. Monroe was a lieutenant, Chiltons, & Ashby's, under the command of Major Leitch, & a like number of troops, from Connecticut, under Col. Knolton, were detached in advance of the army, across the Valley at Haerlem to meet [the British advance]. This small corps met the head of a Column of the enemy at the edge of a wood through which it passed bordering on the valley, & fighting gallantly, checked its career."

—James Monroe, *Autobiography*

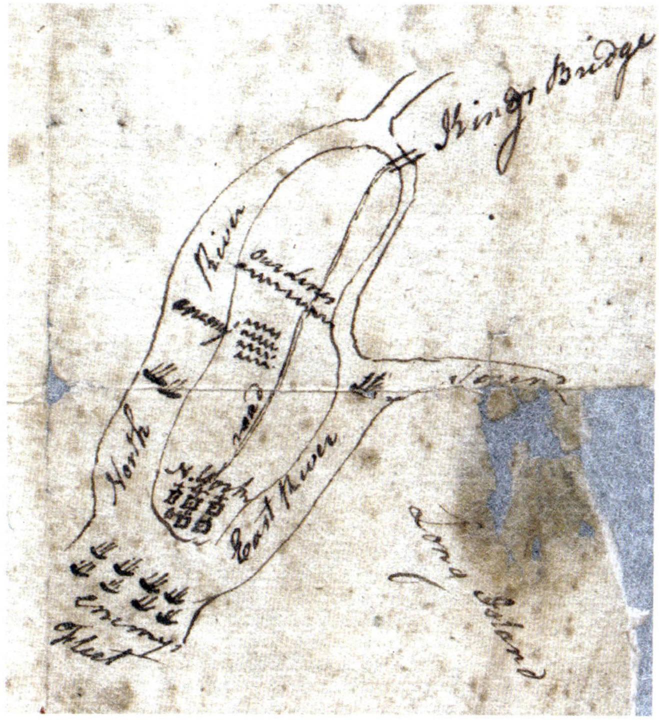

The Third Virginia Regiment joined Washington's army in New York on 13 September 1776 and saw action three days later in the battle at Harlem Heights. John Chilton, a captain in the Third Virginia, drew this sketch of the fight, in which the Americans repulsed a British advance.

Virginia Historical Society, Chilton Papers

A scene from the battle of Monmouth, New Jersey in June 1778. Library of Congress, Prints and Photographs Division

After recovering from his wound, Monroe rejoined Washington's army in August 1777 at the rank of captain and participated in the battles at Brandywine and Germantown, shown at left.

New York Public Library

Upon his return to the army Monroe was assigned to the staff of Major General William Alexander, Lord Stirling and shortly afterwards promoted to major. Monroe remained on Stirling's staff until he resigned from the army in December 1778.

PORTRAIT BY BASS OTIS AFTER AN ORIGINAL BY SIR JOSHUA REYNOLDS, INDEPENDENCE NATIONAL HISTORICAL PARK

Monroe made many new friends during his time in the army, both soldiers and civilians, both men and women. One of these new friends was Catherine Alexander (known as Lady Catherine), the daughter of General Stirling, who later married William Duer.

NEW YORK PUBLIC LIBRARY, EMMET COLLECTION

General Stirling's Headquarters at Valley Forge (Valley Forge National Historical Park). The marker in front of the house reads:

QUARTERS OF MAJOR GENERAL WILLIAM ALEXANDER LORD STIRLING CONTINENTAL ARMY DURING THE VALLEY FORGE ENCAMPMENT DECEMBER 19, 1777–JUNE 19, 1778. MAJOR JAMES MONROE FIFTH PRESIDENT OF THE UNITED STATES ALSO QUARTERED HERE AS AID DE CAMP TO STIRLING

After leaving the Continental Army, Monroe received an appointment as lieutenant colonel in the Virginia service and was assigned to duty at Williamsburg, the state capital. There he met Governor Thomas Jefferson, above, who became his mentor, political ally, and friend.

PORTRAIT BY CHARLES WILLSON PEALE, INDEPENDENCE NATIONAL HISTORICAL PARK

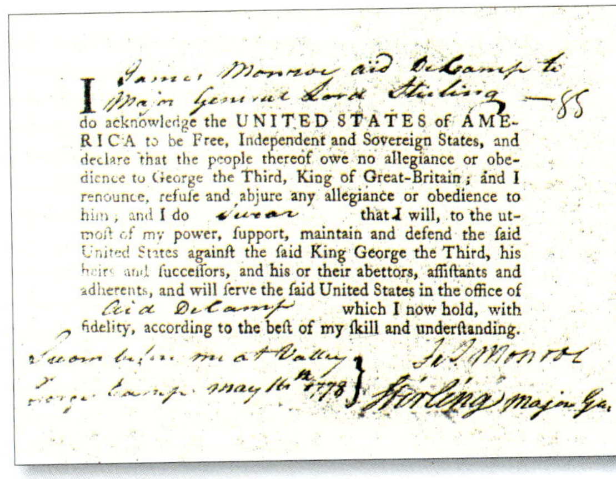

I James Monroe aid DeCamp to Major General Lord Stirling —85
do acknowledge the UNITED STATES of AMERICA to be Free, Independent and Sovereign States, and declare that the people thereof owe no allegiance or obedience to George the Third, King of Great-Britain; and I renounce, refuse and abjure any allegiance or obedience to him; and I do swear that I will, to the utmost of my power, support, maintain and defend the said United States against the said King George the Third, his heirs and successors, and his or their abettors, assistants and adherents, and will serve the said United States in the office of Aid DeCamp which I now hold, with fidelity, according to the best of my skill and understanding.

Sworn before me at Valley Forge Camp May 16th 1778 } Js. Monroe
Stirling Major Gen.

Loyalty oath signed by Monroe while at Valley Forge.

LIBRARY OF CONGRESS, MANUSCRIPT DIVISION, MONROE PAPERS

Monroe did not participate in the siege at Yorktown, but he did see the joint American and French army gathering there and concluded that it would easily defeat the British.

"SURRENDER AT YORKTOWN," LIBRARY OF CONGRESS, PRINTS AND PHOTOGRAPHS DIVISION; ENGRAVING AFTER PAINTING BY JOHN TRUMBULL

THOMAS PINCKNEY

Thomas Pinckney

PORTRAIT BY JOHN TRUMBULL, YALE UNIVERSITY ART GALLERY

In June 1780 Jefferson sent Monroe to North Carolina to observe and report on the advance of the British army. While there, Monroe met Thomas Pinckney, left, of South Carolina. The two men later became political adversaries but remained life-long friends.

"The Executive have occasion to employ a gentleman in a confidential business, requiring great discretion, and some acquaintance with military things. They wish you to undertake it if not inconsistent with your present pursuits."

—THOMAS JEFFERSON TO MONROE, 10 JUNE 1780

"The day after I joined De Kalbs army General Thomas, (then Major) Pinckney, also joined it, & both of us having seen much service, & neither having any command, we moved together, with the small force under De Kalb, about two months lodging in the same quarters every night, and breakfasting & dining together every day. Both of us having been liberally educated, both acting on pure principles, looking to a complete revolution in favor of liberty, our connection was intimate, & friendship sincere."

—MONROE TO GEORGE HAY, 2 MAY 1819

ENTRY INTO GOVERNMENT

JAMES MONROE entered upon his first elected office in April 1782 when he took his seat as a member of the House of Delegates. Monroe served in the assembly only briefly, for two months later his was appointed to the executive council. This body of appointed officials advised the governor and helped him in the administration of the state. Monroe was a member of the council until October 1783, during which time John Marshall and William Short, two of his friends from William and Mary, also served. Most of his time on the council was spent on military matters and defense of the frontier.

Although painted in 1818, this portrait of Monroe by Joseph Castel shows him as a much younger man, perhaps as he may have appeared in the 1780s while serving in Congress. JAMES MONROE MUSEUM

Monroe's term on the council ended when he was elected to the Continental Congress. Congress met in Annapolis, Maryland in December 1783, and Monroe took his seat there alongside his mentor and friend Thomas Jefferson and his army and college friend John Francis Mercer. Monroe arrived in Congress at an auspicious moment, for one of the first events of the session was George Washington's resignation of his commission as commander of the Continental Army. Less than a month later Monroe voted to ratify the Treaty of Paris, which ended the war and by which Great Britain acknowledged the independence of the United States. Not long after that Monroe, Jefferson, and the other members of the Virginia delegation signed the document ceding Virginia's vast territorial claim in the west to Congress.

Monroe had brought a strong interest in the west with

The Virginia General Assembly met in a converted tobacco warehouse in Richmond before the construction of the present capitol. Monroe served in the House of Delegates here when he was first elected to that body in 1782 and again in 1787. LIBRARY OF VIRGINIA

him when he joined Congress. He owned thousands of acres of land in Kentucky and Ohio (both through military bounties and through purchase), and he had worked on western issues as a member of the executive council. He was, therefore, readily inclined to give great attention to that region. The acquisition of the western country meant that Congress had to arrange for its government and defense, and Monroe devoted much of his remaining two years in Congress to these questions. One problem facing the members of Congress was that none of them had been west of the mountains. Monroe sought to remedy this problem by traveling to the west during the summer of 1784. His plan was to travel through New York to Lake Erie, cross the lake to Detroit, and then return home to Virginia by way of Ohio and Kentucky. He made it as far as the shore of Lake Erie (near present-day Buffalo)—seeing Niagara Falls along the way—but the danger of Indian attack forced him to abandon the rest of his journey. Instead he turned northeastward, traveling across Lake Ontario and then down the St. Lawrence River to Montreal. From there he journeyed south to Lake Champlain and then back down the Hudson River to New York.

Monroe was elected to the Continental Congress and joined that body when it convened at the Maryland State House in Annapolis in December 1783. The first event that he witnessed was the resignation of George Washington as commander of the army. John Trumbull's painting of the scene shows Monroe seated in the back row, behind Thomas Jefferson.

Yale University Art Gallery

The Maryland State House.

Library of Congress, Prints and Photographs Division

Congress moved to New York in January 1785, meeting in Federal Hall, shown above at the end of the street.

Library of Congress, Prints and Photographs Division

The following summer he fulfilled his wish of seeing the west when he traveled from Virginia to central Kentucky.

Congress spent the 1784–1785 session at Trenton, New Jersey, and the 1785–1786 session in New York City. During this time Monroe gave considerable attention to the government and defense of the west. In May 1786 he introduced a plan of government for the western country that eventually evolved into the Northwest Ordinance of 1787. While Congress was wrestling with the question of how to govern the western country, another issue arose that, in Monroe's eyes, posed a major threat to the region. In August 1785 John Jay, the American secretary for foreign affairs, began negotiations with Spain to determine the boundary between the United States and the Spanish territory to the south. The following May Jay reported that Spain would sign a commercial treaty with the United States if the United States would forego navigation rights on the Mississippi River for twenty-five years. This set off an extensive debate in Congress, with the northeastern states favoring the proposal and the southern states opposing it. Monroe became a leader of the opposition, and although the issue was not settled until after he left Congress in October 1786, the opposition succeeded in killing the proposal. Monroe's leadership on this matter marked him as an advocate of western interests, a reputation that provided him strong support in the west throughout his long political career.

Monroe first met James Madison when Monroe was a member of the Continental Congress and Madison was in the House of Delegates. Although they were for the most part friends and allies, a rivalry between the two occasionally led to rifts in their friendship.

portrait by Chares Willson Peale, Library of Congress, Rare Books Division

ENEMIES

Monroe met many men during his time in Congress who would be life-long friends and allies, but he met others who would remain adversaries. Monroe had an uneasy relationship with Rufus King, a delegate from Massachusetts and later a leader of the Federalists. Although they were friendly with each other, Monroe never trusted King politically.

Monroe's greatest battle in Congress was fought with John Jay, the American secretary of foreign relations. Jay proposed in 1785 that the United States sign a treaty with Spain that would suspend American rights to navigate the Mississippi River in exchange for commercial rights in Spanish ports. Monroe became a leader of the delegates in Congress who eventually blocked the treaty, a role that made Monroe a hero to the many Americans who were settling in the west.

Rufus King

PORTRAIT BY CHARLES WILLSON PEALE, INDEPENDENCE NATIONAL HISTORICAL PARK

John Jay

PORTRAIT BY GILBERT STUART AND JOHN TRUMBULL, NATIONAL PORTRAIT GALLERY, WASHINGTON

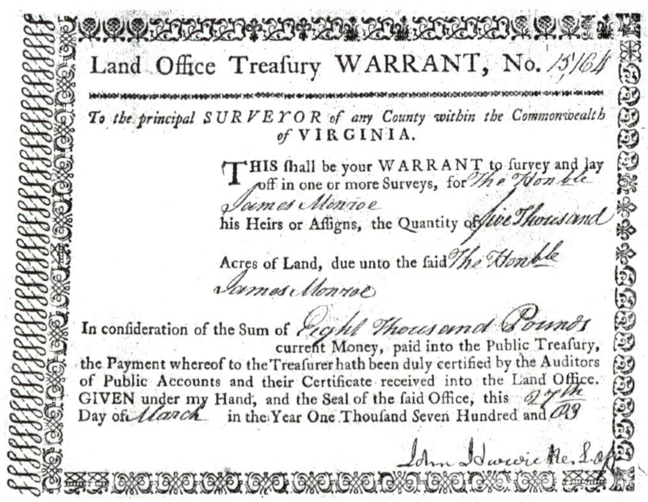

Land Office Treasury WARRANT, No. 15164

To the principal SURVEYOR of any County within the Commonwealth of VIRGINIA.

THIS shall be your WARRANT to survey and lay off in one or more Surveys, for The Honble James Monroe his Heirs or Assigns, the Quantity of Five Thousand Acres of Land, due unto the said The Honble James Monroe

In consideration of the Sum of Eight Thousand Pounds current Money, paid into the Public Treasury, the Payment whereof to the Treasurer hath been duly certified by the Auditors of Public Accounts and their Certificate received into the Land Office. GIVEN under my Hand, and the Seal of the said Office, this 27th Day of March in the Year One Thousand Seven Hundred and 83

John Harvie Re. L.O.

Monroe received land in Kentucky and Ohio as compensation for his service during the Revolutionary War. At the time of his service in Congress he considered leaving Virginia and moving to Kentucky.

KENTUCKY LAND OFFICE DIVISION, FRANKFORT

THE WEST

The western country remained a major topic of discussion throughout Monroe's term in Congress as the delegates debated how best to protect and govern the vast territory west of the mountains. Monroe took a great interest in the west. During the summer of 1784 he set out on a trip with the intention of traveling to western New York, across Lake Erie to Detroit and returning to Virginia by way of Ohio and Kentucky. He made it as far as present-day Buffalo, but had to turn back because of the danger of Indian hostilities. He traveled down the St. Lawrence to Montreal and then back to New York.

Monroe met the great Iroquois leader Joseph Brant in western New York and traveled with him to Montreal.

Joseph Brant

PORTRAIT BY GILBERT STUART
ALNWICK CASTLE, NORTHUMBERLAND, ENGLAND

MAP BY ARROW GRAPHICS

James Monroe

ELIZABETH MONROE

On February 16, 1786 James Monroe married seventeen-year-old Elizabeth Kortright in New York. She was the daughter of Lawrence Kortright, a prosperous but not wealthy merchant, and his wife, Hannah Aspinwall Kortright. She had an elder brother and three sisters.

Monroe, like many of the delegates to Congress, was young and single (he was only twenty-five when he took his seat in Congress). He was one of several delegates who found a wife in New York. And he chose a real beauty. Monroe's cousin and fellow delegate William Grayson wrote to him in November 1785 and reported that the Kortright sisters "made so brilliant and lovely an appearance" at the theater "as to depopulate all the other boxes of all the genteel male people therein."

Another member of Congress described the new Mrs. Monroe as "the little smiling Venus," and when in Paris in the 1790s she was called "la belle américaine." Her personal beauty was accented by her fine sense of fashion, and she was frequently praised for her elegance and style. Louisa Catherine Adams, the wife of John Quincy Adams, noted in 1818 that "she was dressed in white and gold made in the highest style of fashion and moved not like a Queen (for that is an unpardonable word in this country) but like a goddess." Another acquaintance noted that "she is commended exceedingly by those who know her, as a charming and amiable Woman."

She was also a young woman of great spirit, for in October 1786, Elizabeth Monroe, eighteen years old and seven months pregnant, accompanied her husband to their new home in Fredericksburg, Virginia. Years later Monroe complimented her on this, writing that "she left her state & her family, & became a good Virginian."

"It is a remark, which it would be unpardonable to withold, that it was improbable for any female to have fulfilled all the duties of the partner of such cares, and of a wife and parent, with more attention, delicacy and propriety than she has done."
— James Monroe, *Autobiography*

Elizabeth Monroe, painted by Louis Sené in Paris in 1796.

Ash Lawn-Highland, Charlottesville, VA

"The night after you left us our friend Monro was married & next morning decamp'd for Long Island with the little smiling Venus in his Arms, where they have taken house, to avoid fulsome Complements during their first Transports."

—Stephen M. Mitchell to William S. Johnson, 21 February 1786

Elizabeth Monroe by Raphaelle Peale, ca. 1797–1799.

James Monroe Museum

Elizabeth Monroe owned an extensive collection of jewelry. Much of it, like this aquamarine set, was purchased in Paris.

James Monroe Museum

This dress is one of several made for Elizabeth Kortright at the time of her marriage to James Monroe in New York in February 1786.

James Monroe Museum

FREDERICKSBURG

JAMES MONROE'S TERM IN CONGRESS ended in October 1786. He and Elizabeth left New York and traveled to Fredericksburg, Virginia where they made their home. They resided in a house owned by Joseph Jones, and it was there, in November 1786, that their daughter Eliza was born. Monroe wrote to Jefferson and announced the birth, telling him that "Mrs. Monroe hath added a daughter to our society who tho' noisy, contributes greatly to its amusement."

Monroe chose to reside in Fredericksburg because he deemed it a good place to establish his law practice. He purchased a lot at the corner of Charles and William streets (the present site of the James Monroe Museum) and constructed a small building that he used as his office. Although based in Fredericksburg Monroe's practice took him well beyond that town. He practiced in the state court in Richmond and in the district courts at Charlottesville and Staunton. In addition to his private practice he held a commission as the deputy state's attorney at Fredericksburg.

Monroe also remained active in state politics. He stood for election to the House of Delegates in 1786 but lost—he was in New York at the time of the election(his term in Congress not yet having ended), and the voters feared that, having married a New Yorker, he might not return home. He was more successful after his return and won election in both 1787 and 1788, representing Spotsylvania County (the county in which Fredericksburg was located).

The year 1787 was a momentous one for the United States, for during the summer of that year delegates

Patrick Henry was the predominant figure in Virginia politics during Monroe's tenure in the Continental Congress and the state assembly. Henry was governor of Virginia 1784-1786 and a member of the House of Delegates 1787-1790. He was also the leading attorney in the state. He and Monroe were usually on opposing sides in the assembly.

PORTRAIT BY THOMAS SULLY,
COLONIAL WILLIAMSBURG FOUNDATION

meeting in Philadelphia wrote a new constitution. When finished, the delegates sent the document to the states for ratification in special state conventions. Monroe was elected to represent Spotsylvania County at the Virginia convention. Monroe advocated strengthening the national government, and while a member of the Continental Congress had drafted legislation that would have greatly increased the power of the Congress (it was not enacted). He did not, however, approve of the new constitution. He thought that the document was flawed, especially by the omission of a bill of rights. He argued that the national convention ought to reconvene and enact amendments suggested by the state conventions. He was on the losing side, however, for the convention voted in favor of ratification. Monroe acquiesced in the decision and became a staunch supporter of the Constitution once the Bill of Rights was added.

The Monroes resided in a house owned by Joseph Jones on Caroline Street in Fredericksburg. The house, much modified over the years, still stands and is a private residence.

Photograph by Heidi Stello

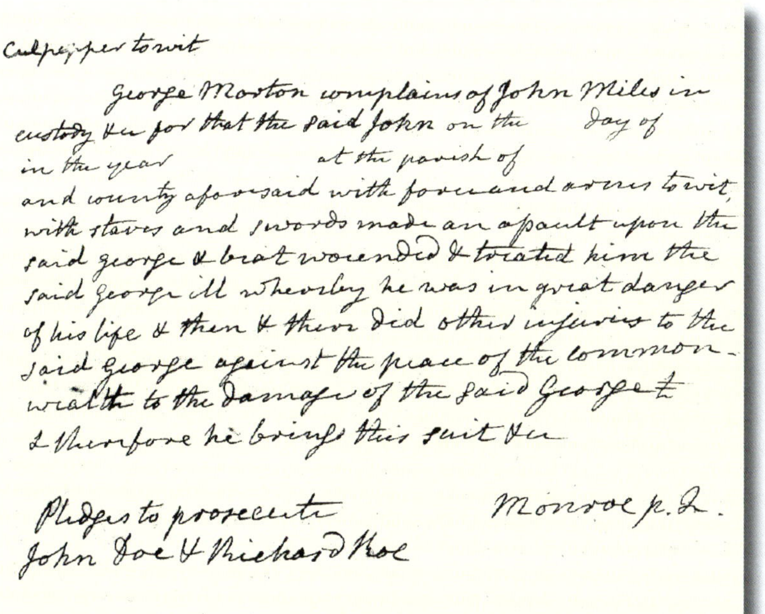

Culpepper to wit

George Morton complains of John Miles in custody &c for that the said John on the day of in the year at the parish of and county aforesaid with force and arms to wit, with staves and swords made an assault upon the said George & beat wounded & treated him the said George ill whereby he was in great danger of his life & then & there did other injuries to the said George against the peace of the common-wealth to the damage of the said George £ & therefore he brings this suit &c

Pledges to prosecute
John Doe & Richard Roe

Monroe p. q.

Monroe was admitted to the bar as an attorney in 1782 but did not commence practice until late 1786. His practice was based in Fredericksburg, but he also appeared in the state courts in Richmond and in the circuit courts in Charlottesville and Staunton. A number of documents relating to cases handled by Monroe, including the complaint shown here, still survive in the records in the court house in Fredericksburg.

Monroe bought a lot at the intersection of William and Charles streets in Fredericksburg in 1786 and constructed a small frame building upon it that he used as his law office. The James Monroe Museum in Fredericksburg occupies a portion of this lot. The original part of the building was constructed in the 1810s, long after Monroe sold the lot.

JAMES MONROE MUSEUM

Fredericksburg was an important port and one of the leading towns in Virginia when the Monroes settled there in 1786. These views are from a diorama that depicts the town as it appeared at the end of the eighteenth century.

KENMORE, GEORGE WASHINGTON'S FREDERICKSBURG FOUNDATION

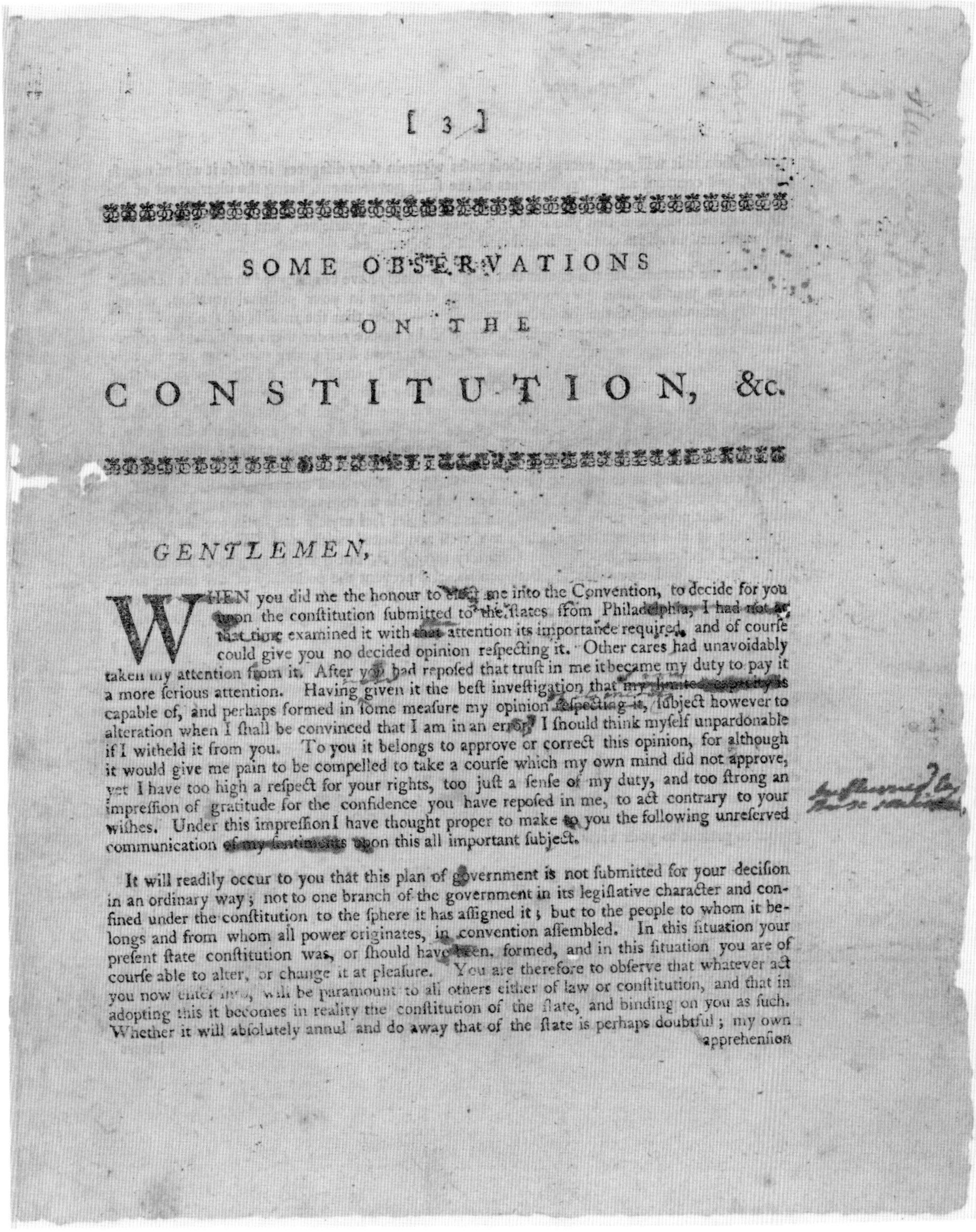

[3]

SOME OBSERVATIONS

ON THE

CONSTITUTION, &c.

GENTLEMEN,

WHEN you did me the honour to elect me into the Convention, to decide for you [illegible] the conſtitution ſubmitted to the ſtates from Philadelphia, I had not at that time examined it with that attention its importance required, and of courſe could give you no decided opinion reſpecting it. Other cares had unavoidably taken my attention from it. After you had repoſed that truſt in me it became my duty to pay it a more ſerious attention. Having given it the beſt inveſtigation that my [illegible] is capable of, and perhaps formed in ſome meaſure my opinion reſpecting it, ſubject however to alteration when I ſhall be convinced that I am in an error, I ſhould think myſelf unpardonable if I witheld it from you. To you it belongs to approve or correct this opinion, for although it would give me pain to be compelled to take a courſe which my own mind did not approve, yet I have too high a reſpect for your rights, too juſt a ſenſe of my duty, and too ſtrong an impreſſion of gratitude for the confidence you have repoſed in me, to act contrary to your wiſhes. Under this impreſſion I have thought proper to make to you the following unreſerved communication of my ſentiments upon this all important ſubject.

It will readily occur to you that this plan of government is not ſubmitted for your deciſion in an ordinary way; not to one branch of the government in its legiſlative character and confined under the conſtitution to the ſphere it has aſſigned it; but to the people to whom it belongs and from whom all power originates, in convention aſſembled. In this ſituation your preſent ſtate conſtitution was, or ſhould have been, formed, and in this ſituation you are of courſe able to alter, or change it at pleaſure. You are therefore to obſerve that whatever act you now enter into, will be paramount to all others either of law or conſtitution, and that in adopting this it becomes in reality the conſtitution of the ſtate, and binding on you as ſuch. Whether it will abſolutely annul and do away that of the ſtate is perhaps doubtful; my own apprehenſion

Monroe recognized the need for and favored measures for the strengthening of the national government, but he was dissatisfied with the constitution that was drafted at Philadelphia. He served as a delegate to the Virginia ratifying convention and voted against ratification, arguing that amendments, including a bill of rights, ought to be made before the plan was enacted. He summarized his views in a pamphlet entitled Some Observations on the Constitution.

Records of the Department of State, National Archives, Washington

James Monroe

U. S. SENATE

IMMEDIATELY AFTER THE RATIFICATION of the Constitution James Monroe and James Madison became opponents for a seat in the new House of Representatives. The campaign was more of a forum on the Constitution than a political contest. The two candidates traveled about the district together, and Madison expounded on the merits of the new government while Monroe called for the addition of a bill of rights.

Madison won, as was expected. In April 1790 Monroe was proposed in the assembly as a candidate for the U. S. Senate, but the position went to another. In November of that year he was once again nominated and this time won. In fact, he was elected twice: once to finish out the last three months of the term of his cousin William Grayson, who had died in office, and then for a full six-year term to succeed Grayson.

Monroe took his seat in the Senate on 6 December 1790 in Philadelphia, which was then the seat of government. Congress was engaged in a bitter debate over the enactment of the economic program proposed by Secretary of the Treasury Alexander Hamilton. Monroe joined the coalition led by James Madison that opposed the measures. This debate raged in the press as well as in the halls of Congress, and Monroe became involved there as well. During the spring and summer of 1792 Hamilton published a series of newspaper essays attacking Thomas Jefferson. They were written over a pseudonym, but everyone knew that Hamilton was the

The new national government initially met in New York, but moved to Philadelphia in December 1790. Monroe took his seat in the Senate at the opening of the first session held in that city. This engraving of Second Street in Philadelphia was made in 1789.

LIBRARY OF CONGRESS, PRINTS AND PHOTOGRAPHS DIVISION

author. Monroe, among others, came to Jefferson's defense, with seven essays that were published during the fall and winter of 1792.

At about this same time, Monroe and Hamilton became involved in a more personal matter. Monroe had been told that Hamilton had been speculating in government funds and was being blackmailed because of it. When he questioned Hamilton about it, Hamilton revealed that he was indeed being blackmailed, not for speculation but because he had been in engaged in an extra-marital affair. Monroe saw this as a private rather than a public matter and took no further interest in it. When news of the affair became public several years later, Hamilton accused Monroe of making it known. Monroe denied it, but Hamilton refused to accept the denial. A duel seemed imminent, but the dispute was resolved without violence.

Another issue of contention stemmed from the outbreak of the revolution in France. At first most Americans applauded the revolution, but when the violence escalated and the king was executed, many Americans abandoned France in favor of the British, who were at war with the French. Monroe was an ardent supporter of the French Revolution and saw the opposition to France as a scheme to forge an alliance with Great Britain and establish a monarchy in the United States. This battle was likewise waged in the press as well as in Congress. In 1791 and again in 1793 Monroe wrote newspaper essays urging the United States to maintain strong ties with the French republic.

Among the new acquaintances Monroe made in Philadelphia was Aaron Burr, a senator from New York. The two became political allies, but Monroe never fully trusted Burr.

PORTRAIT BY JOHN VANDERLYN,
NEW YORK HISTORICAL SOCIETY

Monroe arrived at the capital in the midst of the fight over the fiscal programs of Secretary of the Treasury Alexander Hamilton. Monroe joined the coalition of Congress led by James Madison who opposed Hamilton's measures.

PORTRAIT BY JOHN TRUMBULL,
NATIONAL PORTRAIT GALLERY, WASHINGTON

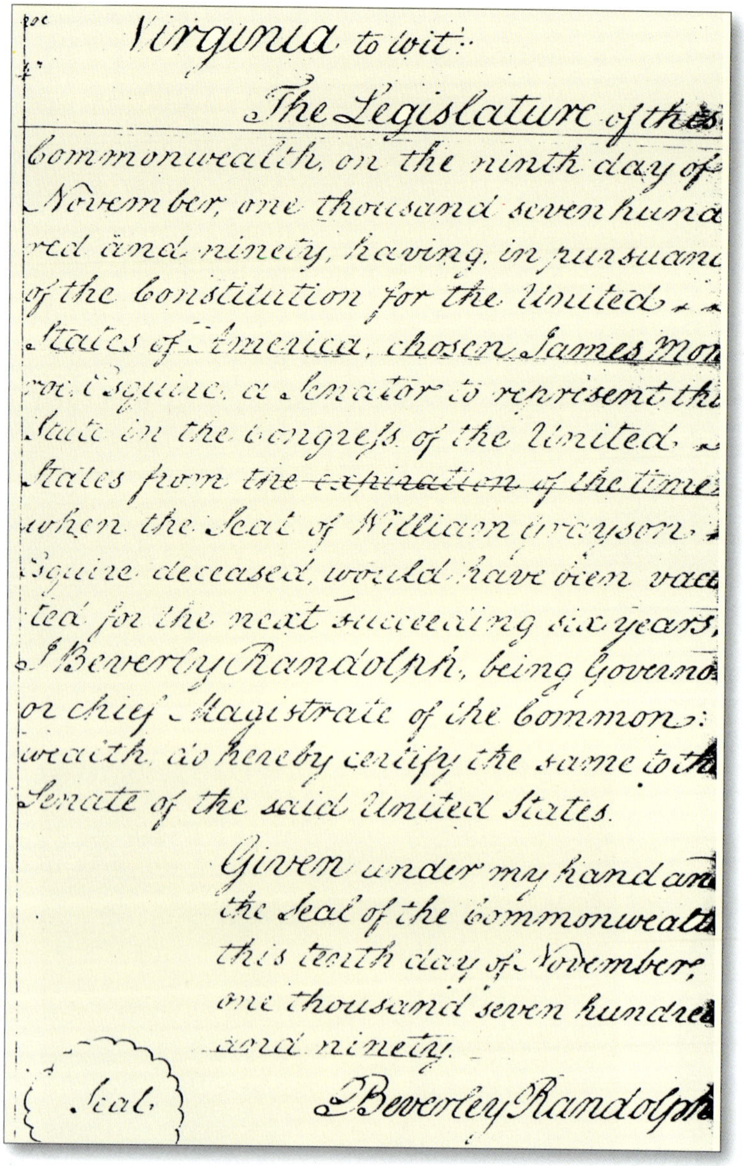

Virginia to wit:

The Legislature of this Commonwealth, on the ninth day of November, one thousand seven hundred and ninety, having, in pursuance of the Constitution for the United States of America, chosen James Monroe Esquire, a Senator to represent this State in the Congress of the United States from the expiration of the time when the Seat of William Grayson Esquire deceased, would have been vacated for the next succeeding six years, I Beverly Randolph, being Governor or chief Magistrate of the Commonwealth do hereby certify the same to the Senate of the said United States.

Given under my hand and the Seal of the Commonwealth this tenth day of November, one thousand seven hundred and ninety.

Seal.

Beverley Randolph

The Virginia assembly appointed Monroe to serve out the last three months of the Senate term of William Grayson (Monroe's cousin) who had died in office. It then elected him to another full six-year term.

Records of the U. S. Senate, National Archives, Washington

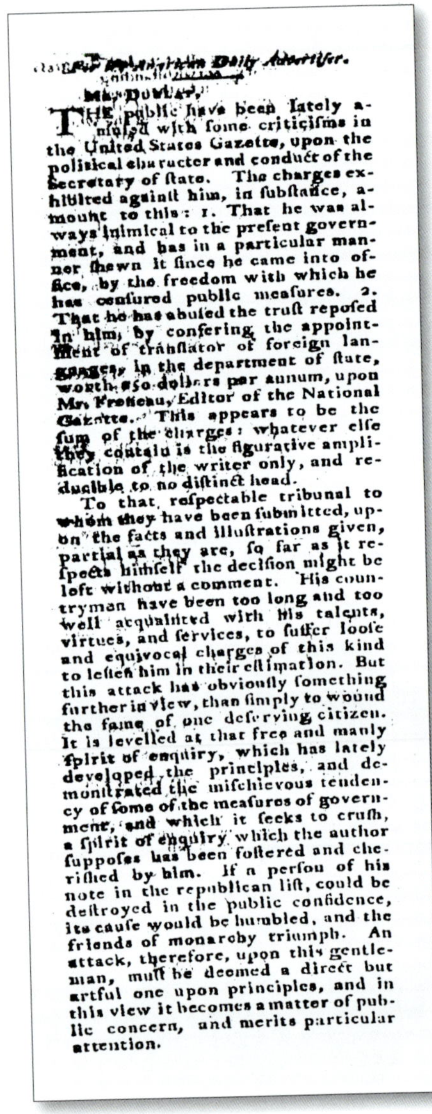

Daily Advertiser.

Mr. Dunlap,

THE public have been lately amused with some criticisms in the United States Gazette, upon the political character and conduct of the Secretary of State. The charges exhibited against him, in substance, amount to this: 1. That he was always inimical to the present government, and has in a particular manner shewn it since he came into office, by the freedom with which he has censured public measures. 2. That he has abused the trust reposed in him, by conferring the appointment of translator of foreign languages, in the department of state, worth 250 dollars per annum, upon Mr. Freneau, Editor of the National Gazette. This appears to be the sum of the charges: whatever else they contain is the figurative amplification of the writer only, and reducible to no distinct head.

To that respectable tribunal to whom they have been submitted, upon the facts and illustrations given, partial as they are, so far as it respects himself the decision might be left without a comment. His countrymen have been too long and too well acquainted with his talents, virtues, and services, to suffer loose and equivocal charges of this kind to lessen him in their estimation. But this attack has obviously something further in view, than simply to wound the fame of one deserving citizen. It is levelled at that free and manly spirit of enquiry, which has lately developed the principles, and demonstrated the mischievous tendency of some of the measures of government, and which it seeks to crush, a spirit of enquiry which the author supposes has been fostered and cherished by him. If a person of his note in the republican list, could be destroyed in the public confidence, its cause would be humbled, and the friends of monarchy triumph. An attack, therefore, upon this gentleman, must be deemed a direct but artful one upon principles, and in this view it becomes a matter of public concern, and merits particular attention.

The political battles of the 1790s were fought in the press as well as in the halls of Congress. Monroe eagerly entered the fray, writing a number of pamphlets and newspaper essays. One series of essays, written under the pen-name "Aratus," urged American support for the French Revolution. Another series of letters defended Thomas Jefferson against criticism leveled by Alexander Hamilton.

Dunlap's American Daily Advertiser, 22 September 1792

James Monroe

MINISTER TO FRANCE

PRESIDENT WASHINGTON appointed James Monroe as minister to France in May 1794. Washington had just appointed John Jay as special envoy to Great Britain, an appointment that alarmed the anti-British Republicans. The president sought to mollify the Republicans (and the French) by sending a minister of known pro-French sentiments to Paris. Monroe had thought that his pro-French and anti-administration positions would have excluded him from any appointment, but Washington chose him for that very reason. Monroe and his family left the United States almost immediately and arrived in Paris on August 2, 1794.

This portrait has long been thought to be one of Monroe, painted in Paris by Louis Sené. It may, however, be his young cousin, Joseph Jones, Jr., who accompanied the Monroes to Paris and attended school there. JAMES MONROE MUSEUM

Monroe arrived in Paris a few days after French revolutionary leader Maximilien Robespierre had been executed. The government was in complete disarray, and there was no executive officer to receive his letter of credence or the letters of friendship that he brought from the president and from Congress. Monroe therefore went to the only effective governing agent—the National Convention—and presented his credentials there. The speech he made, expressing American friendship for France, pleased the French and Monroe's political allies at home, but it outraged the pro-British Federalists, who claimed that it was a breach of American neutrality.

One of the first tasks facing Monroe was to obtain the release of American ships, cargoes, and citizens detained by France. This task was complicated by the disorganization of the French government, but he had some success at it. Very soon after his arrival he was instrumental in obtaining the release of two high profile prisoners: Thomas Paine and Madame de Lafayette. Paine had been invited to France to help write a new constitution, but then, in one of the many contradictions of the revolution, was arrested because he was of English birth. Monroe considered Paine to be a great hero of the American Revolution and successfully petitioned for his release from prison. Madame Lafayette, the wife of General Lafayette, was also in prison in Paris. Lafayette had been

The increasing violence of the French Revolution and especially the execution of King Louis XVI alarmed many Americans, but Monroe and his allies continued to look with favor on the revolution.

Library of Congress,
Prints and Photographs Division

Maximilien Robespierre.

Princeton University Library

a supporter of the revolution in its early stages but grew disenchanted with the cause and tried to flee to America. He was captured by the Austrians (who were at war with France) and imprisoned. Madame Lafayette was arrested and jailed along with other aristocrats in Paris. Their imprisonment became a cause celebre, and many people, including the Monroes, worked for their release. Elizabeth Monroe, in a dramatic scene that brought Madame Lafayette's plight before the public eye, visited her in prison. She was released from confinement in January 1795 and allowed to join her husband in Austria.

In addition to his public duties, Monroe also had to care for his family. At first they resided in a house they rented in Paris and then moved to a house that Monroe bought on the outskirts of the city. The house was a lovely pavilion, and the Monroes furnished it in the best French fashion. Monroe sold the house when he left France and shipped much of the furniture back to Virginia. Eliza Monroe, only seven years old when they arrived in Paris, attended a boarding school kept by Madame Jeanne Louise Henriette Campan, one of the finest schools for girls in France. Fourteen-year-old Joseph Jones, Jr., Monroe's cousin was also with the family, and Monroe enrolled this rather headstrong young man in boarding school as well.

This portrait of Eliza Monroe may have been painted in Paris in 1794. James Monroe Museum

Eliza attended an exclusive boarding school kept by Jeanne Louise Henriette Campan, a former lady-in-waiting at the Court at Versailles.

Ash Lawn-Highland

Monroe's greatest challenge while minister to France was to assure the French government, which felt threatened by a never ending string of plots, both foreign and domestic, to overthrow the revolution, that the United States still valued its alliance with France and that it would remain neutral in the war between France and Great Britain. His effort received a serious check in November 1794 when John Jay, the American envoy to Great Britain, signed a treaty with that nation. The French saw this treaty as confirmation of their suspicions that the Washington administration was pro-British. Monroe was able to prevent an open breach between the United States and France, but he was never able to alleviate the fear that the United States had abandoned its ally. Federalist secretary of state Timothy Pickering blamed Monroe for the deteriorating situation, and President Washington sent a letter of recall in August 1796. The break became official when Monroe left France in January 1797, and the French

Relations between the United States and France deteriorated badly following the signing of the Jay Treaty in 1794. President Washington and his secretary of state, Timothy Pickering, blamed Monroe for the situation and recalled him in 1796.

Timothy Pickering

BY CHARLES WILLSON PEALE
INDEPENDENCE NATIONAL HISTORICAL PARK

refused to receive a new minister to replace him. The Federalists condemned Monroe's mission as a failure, but the Republicans greeted him as a returning hero, with Jefferson and Madison meeting him at the dock. Monroe bridled at the accusations and responded by publishing a pamphlet entitled *A View of the Conduct of the Executive* in which he defended his own conduct and blamed the pro-British policies of the Washington administration for the break with France.

George Washington

BY GILBERT STUART
U.S. SENATE

Thomas Paine, the author of Common Sense *and* The Rights of Man, *was in prison in France when Monroe arrived in Paris. Monroe considered Paine to be a hero of the American Revolution and persuaded the French to release him. Paine resided with the Monroes after his discharge from prison while he recovered his health.* Library of Congress, Prints and Photographs Division

Madame Lafayette
Lafayette College Library, Easton, PA

Monroe purchased a house on the outskirts of Paris for a family residence. This is a conceptual arrangement of one of the salons, using furniture that the Monroes bought in Paris. The portrait in the foreground of Elizabeth Monroe was painted years later. James Monroe Museum

PARIS HOUSE

Mary Pinckney, the wife of Charles Cotesworth Pinckney, who was appointed to succeed Monroe as minister to France, wrote a description of the Monroe house: "Their house is a little temple. It was built by a farmer general in a beautiful style of architecture, and stands in the midst of 20 arpens laid out in terraces and alleys. After ascending a high flight of steps of great length you enter a vestibule, & then, strait on, a small eating room, ornamented with large bronze statues—on each side is a beautiful octagon saloon, profuse with gilding, the finest glasses, painted ceilings, and compartments over the windows."

Mary Pinckney to Gabriel Manigault, 18 December 1796

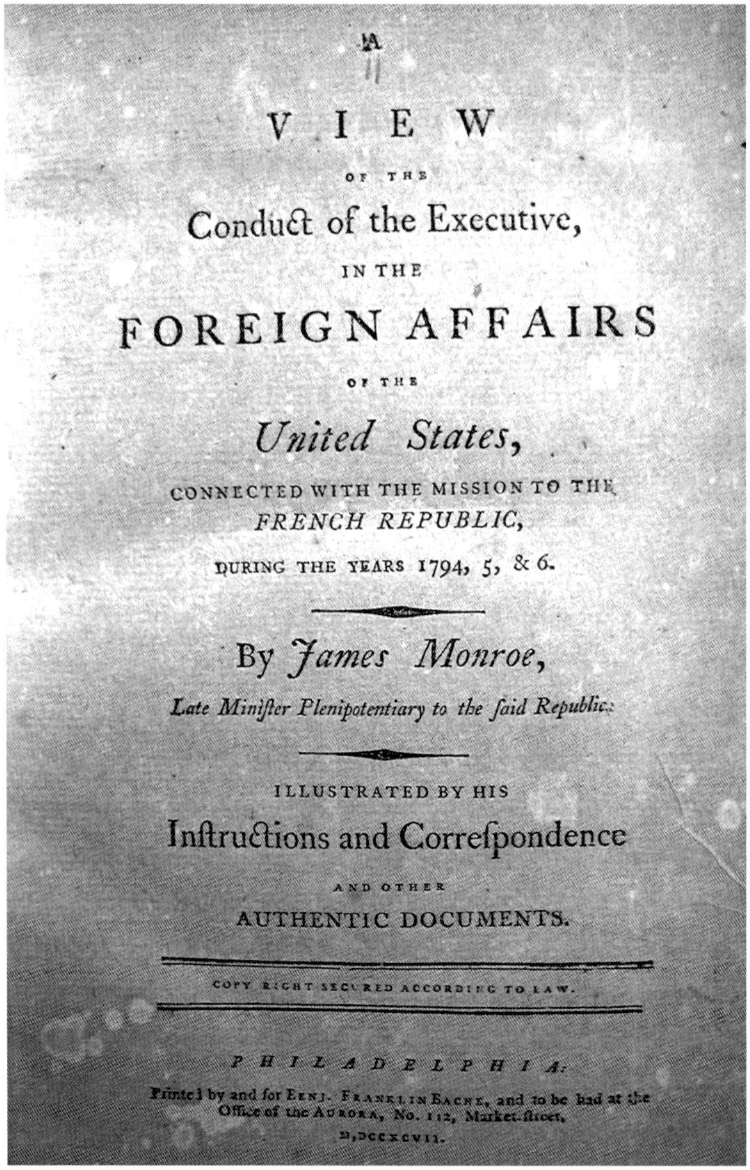

A

VIEW

OF THE

Conduct of the Executive,

IN THE

FOREIGN AFFAIRS

OF THE

United States,

CONNECTED WITH THE MISSION TO THE

FRENCH REPUBLIC,

DURING THE YEARS 1794, 5, & 6.

By *James Monroe,*

Late Miniſter Plenipotentiary to the ſaid Republic:

ILLUSTRATED BY HIS

Inſtructions and Correſpondence

AND OTHER

AUTHENTIC DOCUMENTS.

COPY RIGHT SECURED ACCORDING TO LAW.

PHILADELPHIA:

Printed by and for BENJ. FRANKLIN BACHE, and to be had at the Office of the AURORA, No. 112, Market-ſtreet,

M,DCCXCVII.

Upon his return to the United States in 1797 Monroe published a pamphlet entitled A View of the Conduct of the Executive *that defended his conduct as minister to France and blamed the policies of the Washington administration for the break in relations between the two nations.* James Monroe Museum

James Monroe

HIGHLAND

THE MONROES LEFT FREDERICKSBURG in August 1789 and moved to a farm in Albemarle County. Monroe had long thought of moving west and had even considered settling on the land he owned in Kentucky. It was Jefferson's constant urging that persuaded him. "I wish to heaven you may continue in the disposition to fix [your residence] in Albemarle," Jefferson had written in 1786. "Short will establish himself there, & perhaps Madison may be tempted to do so. This will be society enough, & it will be the sweetener of our lives." The farm was just outside Charlottesville, on land now occupied by the University of Virginia. The soil here was inferior, however, and in 1793 Monroe bought another farm adjacent to Monticello. This property became his home until 1826. Monroe eventually named the farm Highland, and today it is known as Ash Lawn-Highland (combining Monroe's name with a later name for the farm), a historic house museum dedicated to Monroe's memory.

Monroe's departure for France prevented him from occupying the place immediately, although it was farmed during his absence under the direction of his uncle, Joseph Jones. Jefferson drew up plans for a house, and Monroe began construction upon his return to the United States in 1797. The Monroes moved in November 1799. The house was small and was intended to be a temporary residence until a larger one could be built. Monroe's continual absence prevented a second house from ever being built. Despite its small size, the house was elegantly furnished with the fine furniture that the Monroes brought back from France.

Monroe's residence here only partly fulfilled Jefferson's dream of gathering his friends about him. William Short bought a farm adjoining Monroe's on the south (Monticello was to the north), but he never lived there, preferring a residence in Philadelphia instead. Another friend, Philip Mazzei, also owned a farm in the neighborhood but abandoned it and returned to Europe. Madison, happy with his residence in nearby Orange County, remained there. Monroe, however, did have his family about him. His brother Joseph spent much time there, as did his daughter Eliza when she was grown and married. His other brother Andrew and his family resided on an adjacent farm owned by Monroe.

Monroe was very interested in farming, but his frequent absences prevented him from improving the property to the extent he wished. He had to rely on hired farm managers, but that was never a satisfactory arrangement, and the farm was never as profitable as it could have been. Monroe employed a workforce of about fifteen slaves, using them to grow tobacco, wheat, and corn, and to raise sheep. He also had an extensive orchard and a vineyard.

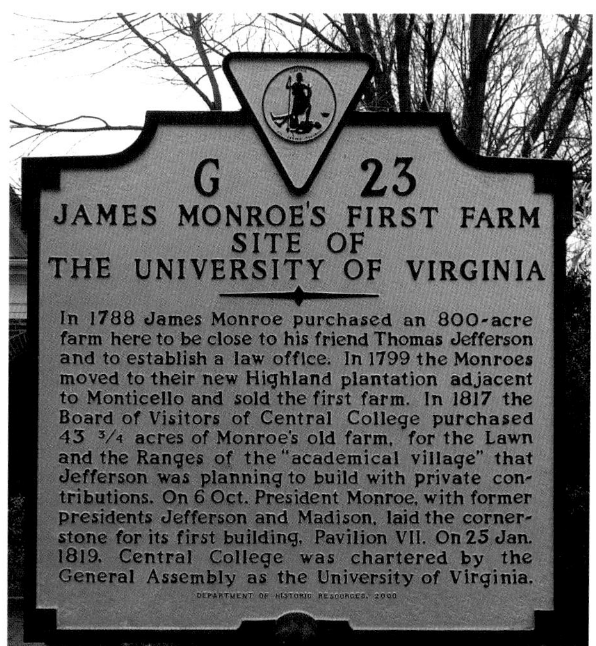

PHOTO BY HEIDI STELLO

The Monroes left Fredericksburg in 1788 and moved to a farm outside of Charlottesville on a site now occupied by the University of Virginia. The small house in which they resided has been incorporated into a large building called Monroe Hill. "We live in two small offices," Monroe wrote in 1798, "and can scarcely say that we are comfortable."

Library of Congress, Prints and Photographs Division

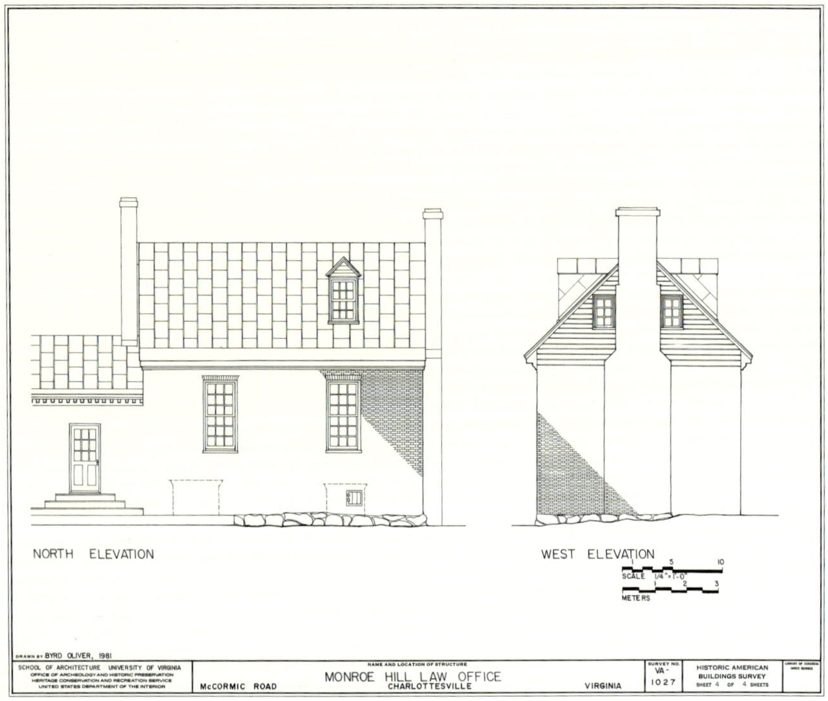

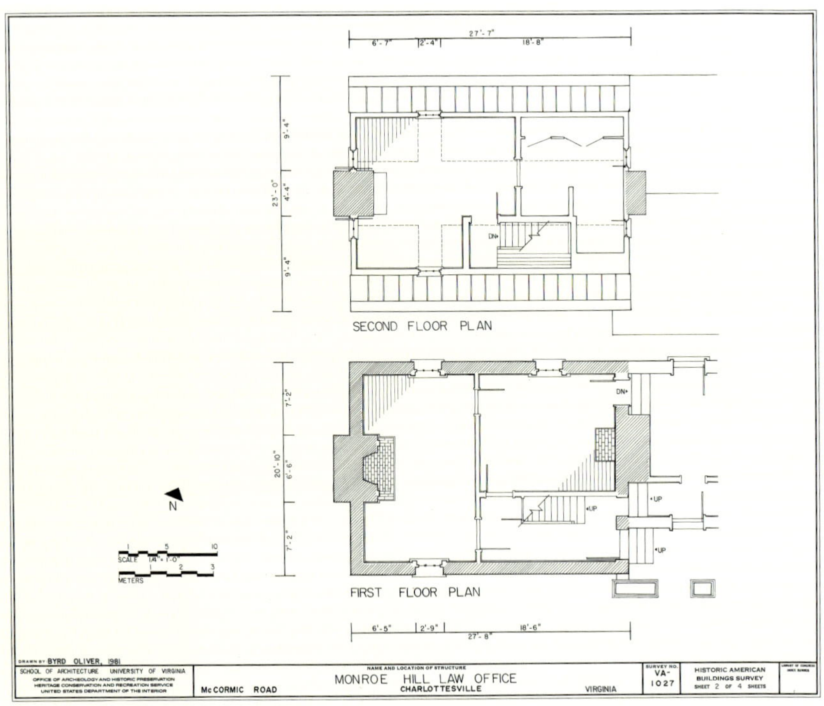

The Monroes moved to a new farm in Albemarle County (which they named Highland in 1818) in 1799. The small white house is the Monroe residence; the larger yellow house was built in the 1870s. The row of dependencies to the right was built by Monroe.

Ash Lawn-Highland

View of the road leading to the house. Ash Lawn-Highland

GENTLEMAN FARMER

"3500 acres about 2000 of which are the best mountain quality. . . . It is five miles from Charlottesville and six from the University. Of its advantageous situation for health and society, no remark need be made here. The estate has all the usual improvements on it, a commodious dwelling house, buildings for servants, and other domestic purposes, good slaves, two barns with threshing machine, a grist and sawmill with good houses for managers and laborers, well noted for each purpose, and all in good repair. The tract may be divided advantageously, into several parts, and will be so disposed of if desired . . . the furniture and stock may be sold with the land."

—Richmond Enquirer, 5 January 1826

"It is a small unfinished cottage affording accommodation insufficient for our small family. It was intended as a temporary one when built, but our absence and other causes prevented our erecting any other since."

—Monroe to Fulwar Skipwith, 12 June 1810

"I have made some small changes. The three rooms in which the servants lodged below the well, have been finished inside, painted and made habitable for friends. I have a new house with two rooms framed just below the present one, for lodgers."

—Monroe to George Hay, 6 September 1818

The house shown in this nineteenth-century photograph was originally built as servants' quarters but was later converted to guest rooms for visitors. Ash Lawn-Highland

The back of Monroe's house. The door on the basement level leads to the kitchen. Ash Lawn-Highland

Present-day view of the two guest houses and the smoke house. Ash Lawn-Highland

Dining room and study. The furnishings at Ash Lawn-Highland are mostly items owned by the Monroes.

ASH LAWN-HIGHLAND

Many houses had their kitchens in separate buildings. The kitchen at Highland is in the basement.

Photo by Daniel Preston

Master bedroom, above, and daughters' bedroom, below.

Ash Lawn-Highland

Many household activities, such as making soap, took place in the yard behind the house. BENJAMIN BUTTERWORTH, THE GROWTH OF INDUSTRIAL ART

In 1897 the Venezuelan government commissioned the New York sculptor and stone cutter Attilio Piccirilli to craft a statue of Monroe for the main plaza in Caracas. A revolution toppled the government, and the statue was never delivered. It remained at Piccirilli's studio until 1931 when Jay Winston Johns, the then owner of Ash Lawn, purchased it and erected it on the grounds.

ASH LAWN-HIGHLAND

Monroe used a labor force of about fifteen slaves to tend his crops of tobacco, wheat, and corn.

Benjamin Butterworth,
The Growth of Industrial Art

The rolling hillsides of the Virginia piedmont provided good pasture for Monroe's flock of sheep.

The American Farmer's Stock Book

James Monroe

GOVERNOR OF VIRGINIA

JAMES MONROE commenced his first term as governor of Virginia in December 1799. Governors were elected by the assembly to a one-year term and could serve three consecutive terms. Monroe, as was common, held office for three years.

Virginia's new capitol, which had been designed by Thomas Jefferson, had been completed the year before Monroe took office. Two other important state building projects were completed during Monroe's term. One was a state penitentiary. Confinement in a penitentiary was introduced as a reform—many crimes that had been previously punished by corporal punishments such as whipping, branding, or hanging were now punished by long-term incarceration. The Virginia penitentiary, which was a model institution, received its first prisoners in early 1800. The second building was a state armory. Virginia was in the process of providing its militia with new arms, and Monroe spent many hours working on contracts for the purchase of muskets, swords, and other weapons. With the completion of the armory in 1802 Virginia began to manufacture these weapons rather than purchase them.

The administration of these new undertakings occupied much of Governor Monroe's time and bordered on routine, but Monroe's term actually began with a major crisis, the aftermath of which continued through to the end of his term. In August 1800 a farmer residing just north of Richmond discovered a plot among local slaves to mount a rebellion. Led by a slave named Gabriel, the conspirators plotted to attack Richmond, capture Monroe and other leading citizens, and hold them hostage until the slaves were given a boat that would allow them to leave the United States. Warned of the plot, Monroe called out the militia and arrested the conspirators. Twenty-seven conspirators, including Gabriel, were hung, and others were subjected to lesser punishments.

Richmond as it appeared when Monroe was governor. The new state capitol, which was completed in 1798, dominated the landscape.

BENJAMIN HENRY LATROBE, MARYLAND HISTORICAL SOCIETY

Monroe oversaw the completion of Virginia's first penitentiary, located in Richmond, and shown here in a drawing by its architect, Benjamin Henry Latrobe. Virginia Historical Society

Monroe oversaw the completion of a new facility in Richmond for the manufacture of muskets, pistols, swords, and other arms for the use of the militia. This musket was made in Richmond in 1802.

Virginia Historical Society

Fears of incipient revolt lingered, and in 1802 another plot was uncovered, which was also quickly suppressed. White Virginians were alarmed by these plots, and some, including Monroe, saw them as a warning of the danger to come unless slavery was ended. Monroe corresponded with Jefferson about the possibility of emancipating the slaves and settling them somewhere outside the United States. This plan was dropped for the time being when no appropriate location for resettlement could be found.

This was also a time of great personal tragedy for the Monroes. Their second child, a boy named James Spence Monroe, was born in May 1799. The child became seriously ill during the summer of 1800 and on September 28, only days before Gabriel went to the gallows, James Spence Monroe died. The Monroes were devastated, but the great turmoil within the state prevented the governor from withdrawing for a period of mourning with his family. James and Elizabeth had feared that this would be their last child, but in 1802 their third and last child, daughter Maria Hester, was born.

Monroe's term in office was also a period of great triumph, for in March 1801 Thomas Jefferson became president of the United States. Monroe and the other Republicans had long chafed under the Federalist control of the national government. Their hope that Federalist power was about to end received a serious check when the tie in the electoral vote between Jefferson and Burr threw the election into the Federalist-dominated House of Representatives. Some Virginia Republicans, fearing that the Federalists would subvert the election and select one of their own to be president, urged Governor Monroe to call the assembly into special session and to put the militia on alert. Monroe, trusting that the House would maintain the Constitution, urged patience. The peaceful outcome of the crisis and Jefferson's election provided both relief and immense satisfaction.

Governor Monroe and other Virginians eagerly anticipated the election of Thomas Jefferson as president. Monroe carefully monitored the proceedings of the House of Representatives as it attempted to resolve the disputed election.

PORTRAIT BY REMBRANDT PEALE, 1805; NEW YORK HISTORICAL SOCIETY

GOVERNOR MONROE

The [Governor] of this Commonwealth is the same [man] who was, not many years ago, the [minister] at Paris. His present office is sufficient evidence of the estimation in which he is held by his native state. In his stature, he is about the middle height of men, rather firmly set, with nothing further remarkable in his person, except his muscular compactness and apparent ability to endure labour. His countenance, when grave, has rather the expression of sternness and irasibility; a smile, however, (and a smile is not unusual with him in a social circle,) lights it up to a very high advantage, and gives it a most impressive and engaging air of suavity and benevolence. Judging merely from his countenance, he is between the ages of forty-five and fifty years. His dress and personal appearance are those of a plain and modest gentleman.

—William Wirt, The Letters of a British Spy, 1803

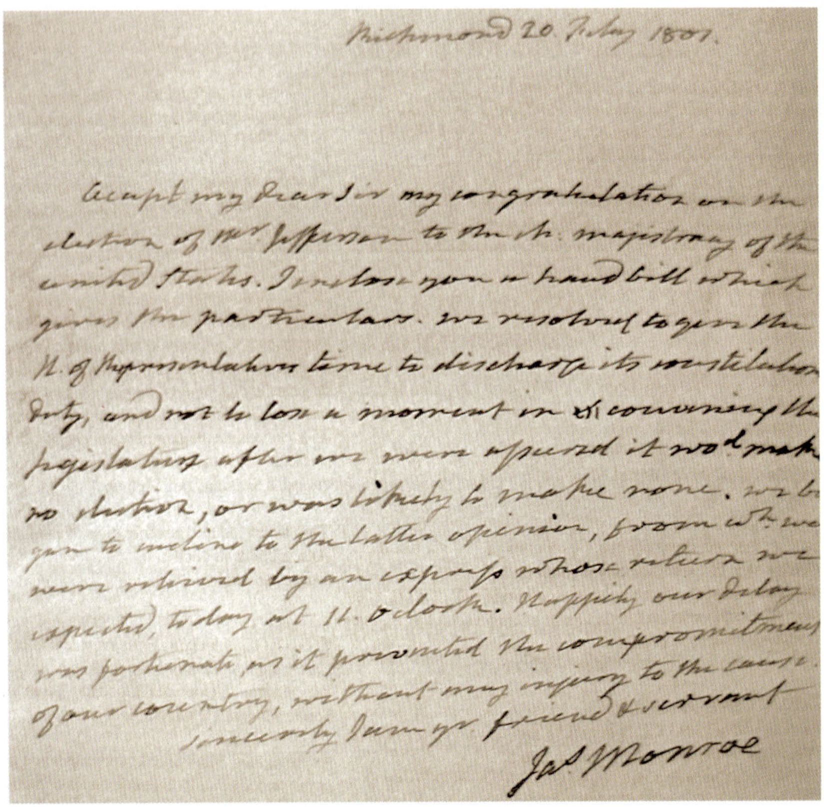

Richmond 20. Feby 1801.

Accept my dear Sir my congratulation on the election of Mr Jefferson to the ch. magistracy of the united States. I inclose you a hand bill which gives the particulars. we resolved to give the H. of Representatives time to discharge its constitutional duty, and not to lose a moment in convening the legislature after we were assured it wod make no election, or was likely to make none. we begun to incline to the latter opinion, from wh we were relieved by an express whose return we expected, to day at 11. o'clock. Happily our delay was fortunate as it prevented the compromitment of our country, without any injury to the cause. sincerely I am yr. friend & servant

Jas Monroe

Monroe expressed his satisfaction and relief in a letter written shortly after he learned of Jefferson's election.

New York Historical Society, Gilder Lehrman Collection

"I have no hesitation to declare, that I consider the late election to the Executive of the United States, as having essentially contributed to secure to us the enjoyment of the blessings for which we contended in our revolution."

—Annual message to the Virginia General Assembly, 7 December 1801

Historic highway signs mark the sites of places associated with Gabriel's Rebellion.

HENRICO COUNTY, VIRGINIA, DEPARTMENT OF PARKS AND RECREATION, PHOTOS BY DAN PRESTON AND LAURA SUMMERS

Amidst the turmoil of Gabriel's Rebellion the Monroes suffered the personal tragedy of the death of their eighteen-month-old son. The boy was buried in St. John's churchyard, pictured here as it appeared in 1836.

ST. JOHN'S CHURCH, RICHMOND

Maria Hester Monroe, the Monroes' third and last child, was born in Richmond in April 1802.

PLASTER RELIEF MADE IN 1820 BY PIETRO CARDELLI, JAMES MONROE MUSEUM

James Monroe

THE LOUISIANA PURCHASE

JAMES MONROE planned to return to his law practice after completing his term as governor, and even placed a notice in the Richmond newspaper announcing his intention. These plans were short-lived, however, for within a month of leaving the governorship, President Jefferson appointed him special envoy to France.

The United States had always been unhappy with the Spanish occupation of the city of New Orleans, which controlled the trade on the Mississippi River. Dissatisfaction turned to alarm in 1802 when it became known that Spain had ceded the vast Louisiana country, which included New Orleans, to the much more powerful and much more aggressive French. President Jefferson immediately instructed Robert R. Livingston, the American minister in Paris, to offer to buy New Orleans or some other tract of land that would assure American access to the mouth of the river. By the end

New Orleans in 1803. CHICAGO HISTORICAL SOCIETY

of the year Jefferson had come to fear that Livingston would not succeed in this endeavor, and decided to send a special envoy to assist in the negotiations. Jefferson believed that Monroe, who had experience as minister to France and who was still remembered for his efforts to protect American rights to the Mississippi in the 1780s, was the right man for the job.

Monroe and his family sailed from New York March 8, 1803 and arrived in Paris on April 12. Immediately upon his arrival Monroe learned that Napoleon, who had been resisting Livingston's overtures, had suddenly reversed himself and offered to the sell to the United States not only New Orleans, but the whole of Louisiana. Monroe and Livingston set to work with François Barbé-Marbois, the French minister of the treasury who had been entrusted with the negotiation, and by the end of April signed the treaty for the transfer of Louisiana.

Republicans such as Monroe and Jefferson were ambivalent on the question of whether Napoleon was a tyrant or not. They had no doubt, however, that his possession of New Orleans was a problem for the United States.

Library of Congress,
Prints and Photographs Division

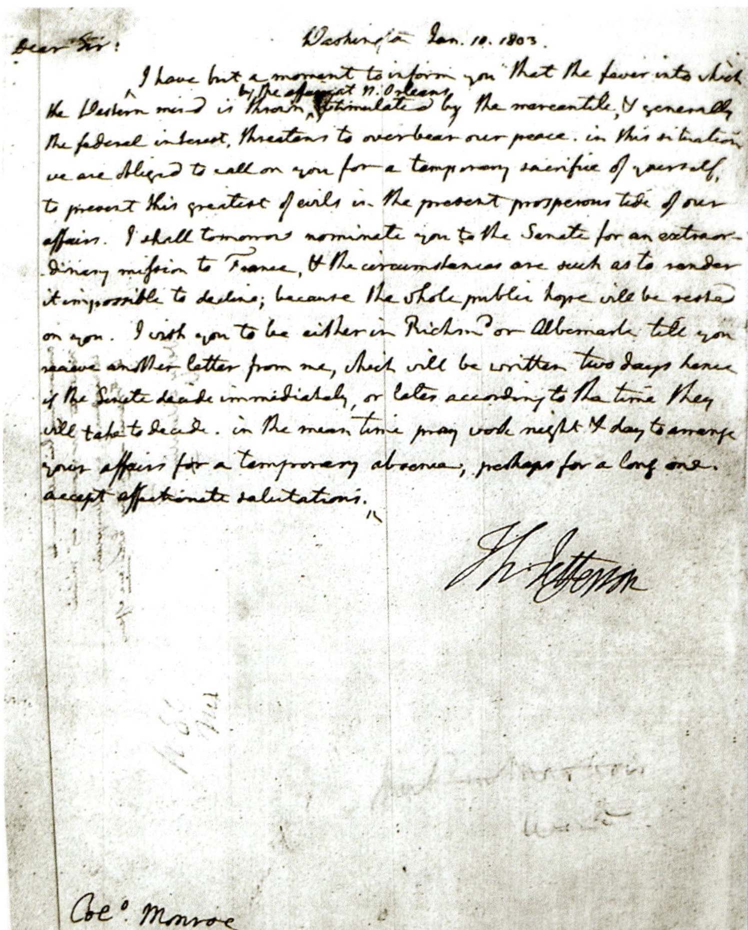

Washington Jan. 10. 1803.

Dear Sir:

I have but a moment to inform you that the fever into which the Western mind is thrown by the affair at N. Orleans, stimulated by the mercantile, & generally the federal interest, threatens to overbear our peace. in this situation we are obliged to call on you for a temporary sacrifice of yourself, to prevent this greatest of evils in the present prosperous tide of our affairs. I shall tomorrow nominate you to the Senate for an extraordinary mission to France, & the circumstances are such as to render it impossible to decline; because the whole public hope will be rested on you. I wish you to be either in Richmd. or Albemarle till you recieve another letter from me, which will be written two days hence if the Senate decide immediately, or later according to the time they will take to decide. in the mean time pray work night & day to arrange your affairs for a temporary absence; perhaps for a long one. accept affectionate salutations.

Th: Jefferson

Col. Monroe

Jefferson wrote to Monroe on January 10, 1803 asking him to go to France to assist in the negotiations for the acquisition of New Orleans.

Library of Congress,
Manuscript Division, Monroe Papers

Sculptor Karl Bitter's monument to the Louisiana treaty at the 1904 St. Louis world's fair (The Louisiana Purchase Exposition) featured a rendering of the signing of the treaty. A bronze version of Bitter's sculptural group is on the grounds of the Missouri state capitol in Jefferson City. Missouri State Archives

François Barbé-Marbois, the French minister of the treasury, knew both Livingston and Monroe from when he was in the United States in the 1780s. Napoleon entrusted him with the negotiation of the Louisiana treaty.

FINE ARTS MUSEUM OF SAN FRANCISCO

Robert R. Livingston was U. S. minister to France 1801-1804. He and Monroe had been friends and were allies against the Federalists. Livingston believed that he could have negotiated the Louisiana treaty on his own and resented Monroe's presence.

PORTRAIT BY GILBERT STUART, CLERMONT STATE HISTORICAL SITE, GERMANTOWN, NY

An 1875 fresco of the signing of the Louisiana Treaty

BY CONSTANTINO BRUMIDI IN THE U. S. CAPITOL

The official transfer of Louisiana took place at New Orleans on December 20, 1803.

PAINTING BY THURE DE THULSTRUP, 1903
LOUISIANA HISTORICAL SOCIETY

SONOFTHESOUTH.NET

The Louisiana treaty consisted of three separate documents—a treaty for the transfer of the territory, a convention outlining the details of how payment would be made, and a convention for settling financial claims of American citizens against France. Shown here is Monroe's draft of the convention for arranging payment.

Haverford College Library, Haverford, PA: Roberts Autograph Collection

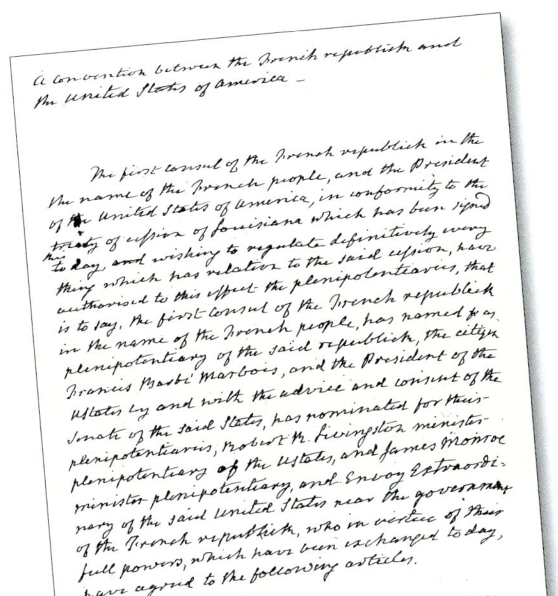

a convention between the French republick and the United States of America _

The first consul of the French republick in the name of the French people, and the President of the United States of America, in conformity to the treaty of cession of Louisiana which has been signed to day, and wishing to regulate definitively every thing which has relation to the said cession, have authorised to this effect the plenipotentiaries, that is to say, the first consul of the French republick in the name of the French people, has named for plenipotentiary of the said republick, the citizen Francis Barbé Marbois, and the President of the UStates by and with the advice and consent of the Senate of the said States, has nominated for their plenipotentiaries, Robert R. Livingston minister plenipotentiary of the UStates, and James Monroe minister plenipotentiary, and Envoy Extraordinary of the said United States near the government of the French republick, who in virtue of their full powers, which have been exchanged to day, have agreed to the following articles.

article 1st

The government of the UStates engages to pay to the French government, in the manner specified in the following article, the sum of sixty millions of Francs, independant of the sum which

James Monroe

U.S. MINISTER TO GREAT BRITAIN

The Monroes found London to be very expensive and disliked living there. British Library

The negotiations with France having been completed, James Monroe left Paris in July 1803 for London to assume the duties of U. S. minister to Great Britain. The outbreak of war between France and Great Britain led to a renewal of depredations on American shipping, as each nation began to intercept American ships bound for the ports of the other. Secretary of State James Madison instructed Monroe to negotiate a new commercial treaty with Great Britain that would protect American neutral shipping rights. He was specifically instructed to obtain a guarantee that Great Britain would end the practice of impressing seamen from American ships.

The war with France created a great demand for seamen in the British navy. Enlistments were inadequate so the navy used impressment (drafting) to fill the ranks. Many British seamen, not wanting to serve in

"I find that my position here [in London] exposes me to greater expence than I had expected, so much as to preclude all hope of deriving any advantage from it. . . . The moisture of the climate and smoak, have given us all colds, & [Mrs. Monroe] is attended with a stricture of the breast, which is an additional reason for us to get home as soon as possible."

—Monroe to Joseph Jones, 12 March 1804

Elizabeth Monroe began to suffer ill health while in England and sought relief by visiting spas such as Bath.

Library of Congress

In addition to his appointment as minister to Great Britain Monroe also bore a commission as special envoy to Spain. He spent the first five months of 1805 in Madrid trying to negotiate the purchase of Florida but was unsuccessful .

University of Texas, Austin,
Perry-Casteñeda Library Map Collection

the British navy, took jobs on American ships, hoping that American neutrality would protect them. British warships, disregarding American neutrality, regularly stopped American vessels and removed seamen—some British, some not—to augment their depleted crews.

An opportunity for a favorable treaty arose in February 1806 when a new British ministry with Charles James Fox as secretary for foreign affairs came to power in London. Fox, unlike most leading British political leaders, was friendly towards the United States and was eager for a resolution of the problems with that country. He appointed Lord Auckland and Lord Holland, who were also well-disposed towards the United States, to conduct the negotiation. The United States, for its part, sent William Pinkney to London to join Monroe in the negotiation. Monroe considered this appointment to be unnecessary, but well aware of the discord that had arisen between himself and Livingston at Paris, was careful not to become resentful towards Pinkney. The commissioners signed a treaty in December 1806 that had the potential to ease tensions between the two countries, but it had one fatal flaw: it did not contain a provision for the ending of impressment. Impressment had become essential to the manning of their navy, and the British absolutely refused to abandon the practice.

The American government was equally adamant on the issue, and when President Jefferson received the treaty he rejected it without even submitting it to the Senate for ratification. Monroe knew that the treaty did not meet his instructions, but he saw it as a first step in protecting American neutral rights, and greatly

President Jefferson appointed William Pinkney of Baltimore as special envoy to assist Monroe in the negotiations with Great Britain. Monroe thought the appointment to be imprudent and unnecessary but, mindful of the strife that had arisen between Robert R. Livingston and himself, took care to remain on friendly terms with Pinkney.

Library of Congress, Prints and Photographs Division

resented Jefferson's rejection of the treaty. The failure of the treaty seemed to signal a deterioration of relations between the two countries, a situation that was worsened by the attack of the British warship *Leopard* on the American frigate *Chesapeake* off the coast of the United States in June 1807. The captain of the *Leopard* had information that several British deserters had enlisted into the crew of the *Chesapeake*. When the captain of the *Chesapeake* refused to surrender these men, the *Leopard* fired upon the *Chesapeake*, killing three American seamen. The British then boarded the American ship and removed the suspected deserters. The United States was of course outraged. The British acknowledged that they were wrong, but the bad feelings between the two nations were so strong that the issue was not resolved until 1811. This crisis marked a final sour note in Monroe's mission to France. Having received permission to return home, he eagerly left England in November 1807.

Monroe's professional frustration was augmented by a dislike of London. The Monroes made many friends while in England—including Lords Auckland and Holland and a distant cousin, Alexander Munro—but they found London to be very expensive and did not like living there. In addition, Elizabeth Monroe suffered from ill health while there; the family spent time at the fashionable spas at Bath and Leamington, but she found no relief. They yearned to return home, but the unsettled state of affairs between the United States and Great Britain delayed their departure until the end of 1807.

In addition to his appointment as minister to Great Britain, Monroe also held a commission as special envoy to Spain. The United States was anxious to acquire the Spanish territory in Florida and along the coast west to New Orleans. Monroe traveled to Spain in late 1805 and joined Charles Pinckney, the American minister in Madrid, in efforts to effect a treaty. The Spanish had no intention of ceding this strategic area, and Monroe spent a fruitless five months pursuing the subject.

While James was in Spain, Elizabeth and young Maria Hester resided with friends near Paris where Eliza was attending her old school at Madame Campan's. Monroe spent time in Paris both before and after his trip to Spain. During his first stay the Monroes attended the great fete in Paris that marked the coronation of Napoleon Bonaparte as emperor of France.

Coronation of Napoleon.
LINDERMAN LIBRARY, LEHIGH UNIVERSITY, BETHELHEM, PA.

The Monroe Museum in Fredericksburg owns the suit that James Monroe wore to the coronation as well as the dress worn by Elizabeth Monroe.

Tension between the United States and Great Britain escalated in June 1807 when the British warship Leopard *stopped the American frigate* Chesapeake *and demanded the surrender of four alleged British deserters. When the captain of the* Chesapeake *refused, the British fired upon the American ship, killing three seamen. The British then boarded the* Chesapeake *and removed the four alleged deserters. Monroe vigorously protested this attack, but the matter was not resolved until 1811.*

MARINERS' MUSEUM, NEWPORT NEWS, VA

The war against France created a great demand for seamen for the British navy. When enlistments proved inadequate the British resorted to impressing (that is, drafting) men into the navy. British warships, seeking to augment their crews, stopped American merchant ships and impressed any seamen they suspected of being British subjects. The United States objected to this violation of its sovereignty and neutrality in the war, but the British turned a deaf ear to the complaints.

GEORGE EASTMAN HOUSE, ROCHESTER, NY

Lord Holland

Portrait by Francois Fabre

Baron Auckland

Portrait by Thomas Lawrence, National Portrait Gallery, London

When Monroe proposed a new treaty between the United States and Great Britain, the British government appointed Baron Auckland and Lord Holland to conduct the negotiations. Both men favored an amelioration of the tension between the two countries and both men became friends with Monroe.

HOLLAND-WOOD

"In thinking more of a name for the cottage as I rode down, Lord Holland occurred to me. He belongs to, perhaps, the most distinguished whig family in England. He has ever been well-disposed to us nationally; cherishing also towards you personally, as is so apparent, sentiments of the greatest kindness. Your connexion with him grew out of your publick employments, a circumstance which will cause it to be adverted to with the more pleasure by your family after you. Holland-place, I do not like; nor Holland-hill, notwithstanding the alliteration. But "Holland-wood" is a fine sonorous compound, fills the ear well, and I like it altogether. Pray call it Holland-wood and tell his Lordship so the next time you write to him."

—Richard Rush to Monroe, 4 September 1816

James Monroe

RETURN TO THE UNITED STATES

For the second time in his career James Monroe returned home from a diplomatic mission disgruntled with the treatment he had received from the government. Monroe believed that the treaty he negotiated with Great Britain offered a real chance for peace between the two countries. His great admiration for Thomas Jefferson prevented him from attaching any blame to the president. Instead, he directed his dissatisfaction at Secretary of State James Madison. Although close friends, Monroe and Madison were also rivals for political advancement, especially for the eventual attainment of the office of president. Monroe came to believe that

James Monroe by Felix Sharples, probably painted between 1807 and 1811.

Independence National Historic Park

This portrait was at one time thought to be James Monroe, but it is most likely his nephew, James Monroe, Jr.

James Monroe Museum

Dissident Republicans in Virginia persuaded Monroe to run against James Madison in the 1808 presidential election. Monroe had no hope of winning and saw the contest primarily as a way to challenge Madison's foreign policy.

PORTRAIT BY GILBERT STUART, COLONIAL WILLIAMSBURG FOUNDATION

Madison, hoping to promote his own political ambitions and to deny Monroe an achievement that would advance his, had been responsible for the rejection of the British treaty. Such suspicions were probably unfounded, but the rivalry was very real. Furthermore, Monroe had come to believe that diplomacy and not economic coercion—the policy favored by Madison—was the best means of settling differences with Great Britain.

Monroe was abetted in his suspicions by dissident Republicans in Virginia who did not trust Madison and who hoped to block his ascent to the presidency. These men persuaded Monroe to enter the 1808 presidential race. Monroe gradually cooled off and did not personally oppose Madison's election. He saw his candidacy as a means of promoting his ideas on how to resolve the crisis with Great Britain. Monroe had no illusion that he would win, and except for writing a few letters explaining his views on foreign relations, made no effort to get elected. In the critical weeks just before the election he left his base in Virginia and traveled to Kentucky to attend to his long-neglected land investments there. Madison won the election, and Monroe had no regrets.

Monroe actually sought a respite from public service at this time so that he could direct his attention to his private affairs, which had suffered during his absence. He spent much of his time supervising work at his farm and trying to get it into good condition. He also contemplated renewing his law practice.

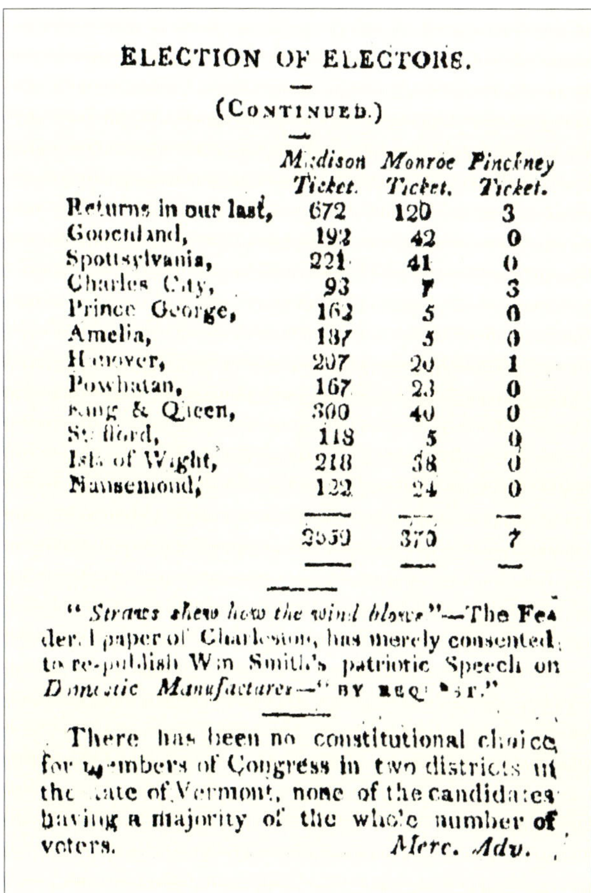

ELECTION OF ELECTORS.

(CONTINUED.)

	Madison Ticket.	Monroe Ticket.	Pinckney Ticket.
Returns in our last,	672	120	3
Goochland,	192	42	0
Spottsylvania,	221	41	0
Charles City,	93	7	3
Prince George,	162	5	0
Amelia,	187	5	0
Hanover,	207	20	1
Powhatan,	167	23	0
King & Queen,	300	40	0
Stafford,	118	5	0
Isle of Wight,	218	38	0
Nansemond,	122	24	0
	2559	370	7

"*Straws shew how the wind blows*"—The Federal paper of Charleston, has merely consented to re-publish Wm Smith's patriotic Speech on *Domestic Manufactures*—"BY REQUEST."

There has been no constitutional choice for members of Congress in two districts in the state of Vermont, none of the candidates having a majority of the whole number of voters. *Merc. Adv.*

Presidential election returns for several Virginia counties.

RICHMOND ENQUIRER, 11 NOVEMBER 1808

It was also a time for family matters. His sister Elizabeth Buckner had died in 1802, his uncle Joseph Jones had died in 1805, and his cousin Joseph Jones, Jr. died in 1808; Monroe gave great attention to settling their affairs. He saw much of his brothers at this time, for both Andrew and Joseph lived near him in Albemarle County. It was also at this time that Monroe formed a close life-long attachment to his nephew, James Monroe, Jr., the son of Andrew. The boy showed a promise of ambition and talent, and the elder Monroe became his patron and a second father to him. And Eliza and Maria continued to be the delight of their parents' life. Monroe wrote that Maria "promises to afford us all the gratification, as she grows up, which parents can expect from a fine child." Eliza grew to be a charming

George Hay was twenty-one years older than Eliza Monroe, but they proved to be a well-matched and companionable couple. Ash Lawn-Highland

James and Elizabeth Monroe made frequent visits to George and Eliza Hay at their house in Richmond .

Mutual Assurance Policy, 1804, Library of Virginia

"Mrs. Hay, whom you know to be remarkably gay and lively, when a girl, is now a retired, sedate and diligent domestic character, delighted only with her own family and the society of her mother and sister."

—Monroe to Fulwar Skipwith, 12 August 1813

Eliza Monroe Hay. Ash Lawn-Highland

young woman, and in September 1808 married George Hay, a prominent Virginia attorney. The following year Hortensia Hay, Eliza's daughter and the Monroes' first grandchild, was born.

Monroe remained out of public service for three years—from November 1807 to December 1810, the longest period in his adult life—but he could not resist the siren song of public affairs forever. He was elected to the House of Delegates, and took his seat in December 1810. His time in the assembly was very short, however, for he was elected governor of Virginia and took office on January 18, 1811. Monroe's fourth term as governor lasted less than three months. In April 1811 President Jams Madison called him to Washington to serve as secretary of state in his cabinet.

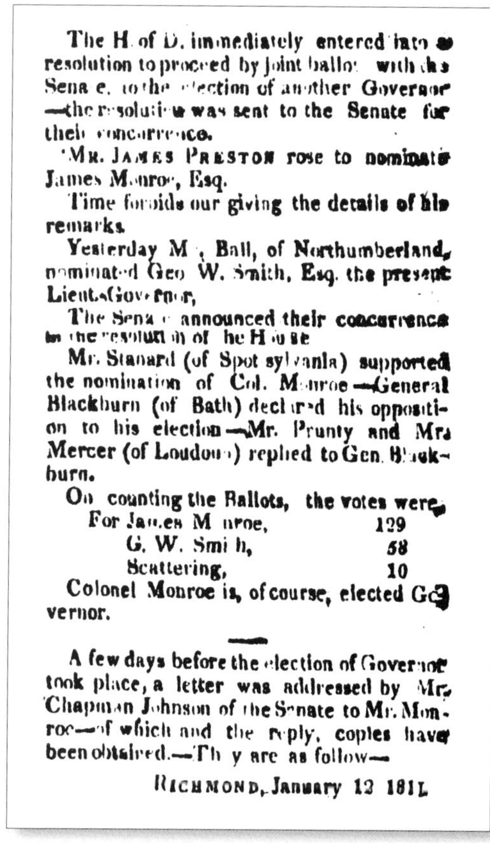

The H. of D. immediately entered into a resolution to proceed by joint ballot with the Senate, to the election of another Governor—the resolution was sent to the Senate for their concurrence.

MR. JAMES PRESTON rose to nominate James Monroe, Esq.

Time forbids our giving the details of his remarks.

Yesterday Mr. Ball, of Northumberland, nominated Geo W. Smith, Esq. the present Lieut. Governor,

The Senate announced their concurrence in the resolution of the House

Mr. Stanard (of Spotsylvania) supported the nomination of Col. Monroe—General Blackburn (of Bath) declared his opposition to his election—Mr. Prunty and Mr. Mercer (of Loudoun) replied to Gen. Blackburn.

On counting the Ballots, the votes were,

For James Monroe,	129
G. W. Smith,	58
Scattering,	10

Colonel Monroe is, of course, elected Governor.

A few days before the election of Governor took place, a letter was addressed by Mr. Chapman Johnson of the Senate to Mr. Monroe—of which and the reply, copies have been obtained.—They are as follow—

RICHMOND, January 12 1811.

RICHMOND ENQUIRER, 17 JANUARY 1811

Monroe served briefly in the Virginia House of Delegates before being elected governor in January 1811. The governor's office was in the capitol. LIBRARY OF VIRGINIA

Drying and threshing wheat.
Benjamin Butterworth,
The Growth of Industrial Art

FARM LIFE

"The truth is that I have become for the first time in my life much engaged & much attached to my farm & to the duties connected with it. I had received from Bordeaux cuttings from vines on all the estates in that quarter, which I had placed in my ground, & which are thriving there. . . . You must not however infer any thing unfavorable to my agricultural acquirements. I can assure you that I had made some improvements in the product & appearance of my property in Albemarle. I had sown much clover seed, & covered the ground with plaister of Paris, & derived considerable advantage from the crop of hay last summer & autumn. I had undoubtedly the best clover in the county, & most ground appropriated to it. My industry was a subject of mirth to the old planters & farmers at the commencement but they had ceased to laugh at my experiments before the end of the year."

—Monroe to William Short, 16 February 1811

Monroe resided at Highland in Albemarle County after his return from London and spent much of his time improving his farm.

Ash Lawn-Highland

Hortense de Beauharnais, whose mother Josephine married Napoleon Bonaparte, attended school with Eliza Monroe at Madame Campan's in Paris. She sent these jewels to Eliza as a present, either for her wedding or for the birth of her daughter, whom Eliza named Hortensia in honor of her friend.

Ash Lawn-Highland

James Monroe

SECRETARY OF STATE & THE WAR OF 1812

James Monroe assumed the duties of secretary of state on April 6, 1811. Madison had originally appointed Robert Smith, a member of a politically influential Maryland family, to that position, but Smith proved to be an unsatisfactory choice. Relations between Monroe and Madison were uneasy at first but in time their friendship was renewed and was as strong as it had ever been.

American relations with Great Britain had not improved in the three years since Monroe had left London. Madison, like Jefferson before him, favored a policy of commercial restriction to force Great Britain to cease its depredations on American shipping. France also infringed American neutral rights, and American policy was likewise directed at effecting an end to French depredations. But Great Britain, with its large and powerful navy, had a greater capability to interfere with American shipping and was therefore seen as the primary offender.

When Monroe became secretary of state he began extensive discussions with Augustus Foster, the British minister to the United States, hoping that diplomatic negotiation would succeed where economic coercion had failed. This attempt proved to be just as fruitless. Great Britain, locked in a deadly contest with France, was not willing to abandon practices that it deemed essential to its war effort. The United States, for its part, had no recourse than to either back down and acquiesce to British policy or to go to war. By spring 1812 Monroe had concluded that war was the only choice left. In April and May 1812 he wrote a series of newspaper essays reviewing American efforts to resolve the problems with Great Britain and presenting the administration's case for going to war. On June 18, 1812 the United States declared war on Great Britain.

The Monroes resided in a brick townhouse at 2017 "I" Street NW in Washington throughout Monroe's tenure as secretary of state. The house is now occupied by the Arts Club of Washington. James Monroe Museum

The war was almost a disaster for the United States. The United States had neither the army nor the supply system necessary to wage a successful war. In addition, opposition to the war was widespread throughout the

James Madison, painted by John Vanderlyn in Washington in 1816. James Monroe commissioned Vanderlyn to paint this portrait.

The White House, Washington

MADISON RECRUITS MONROE

Madison first approached Monroe about serving as secretary of state in mid-March 1811. Monroe signified his willingness to serve in this letter of March 29. Madison issued the commission appointing Monroe on April 2.

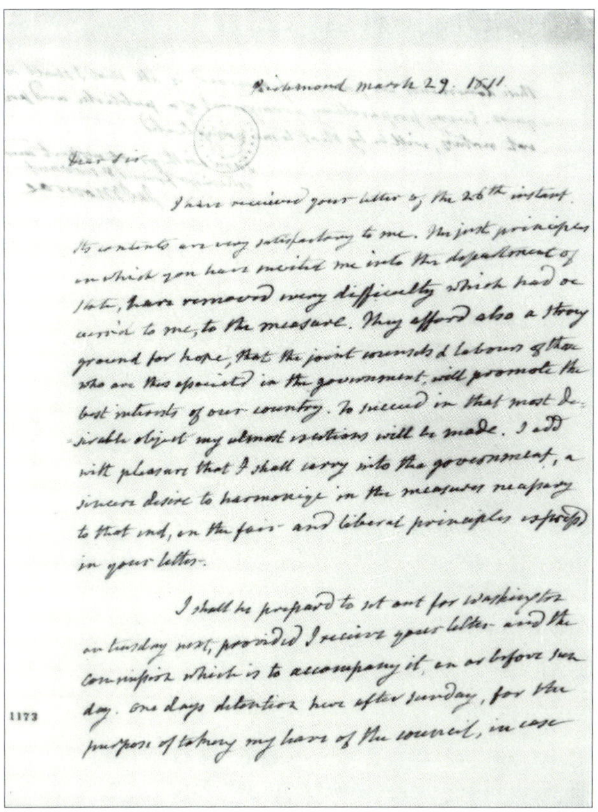

Richmond March 29. 1811

Dear Sir

I have received your letter of the 26th instant. Its contents are very satisfactory to me. The just principles on which you have invited me into the department of State, have removed every difficulty which had occurr'd to me, to the measure. They afford also a strong ground for hope, that the joint counsels & labours of those who are thus associated in the government, will promote the best interests of our country. To succeed in that most desirable object my utmost exertions will be made. I add with pleasure that I shall carry into the government, a sincere desire to harmonize in the measures necessary to that end, on the fair and liberal principles expressed in your letter.

I shall be prepared to set out for Washington on tuesday next, provided I receive your letter and the commission which is to accompany it, on or before that day. One days detention here after sunday, for the purpose of taking my leave of the council, in case

1173

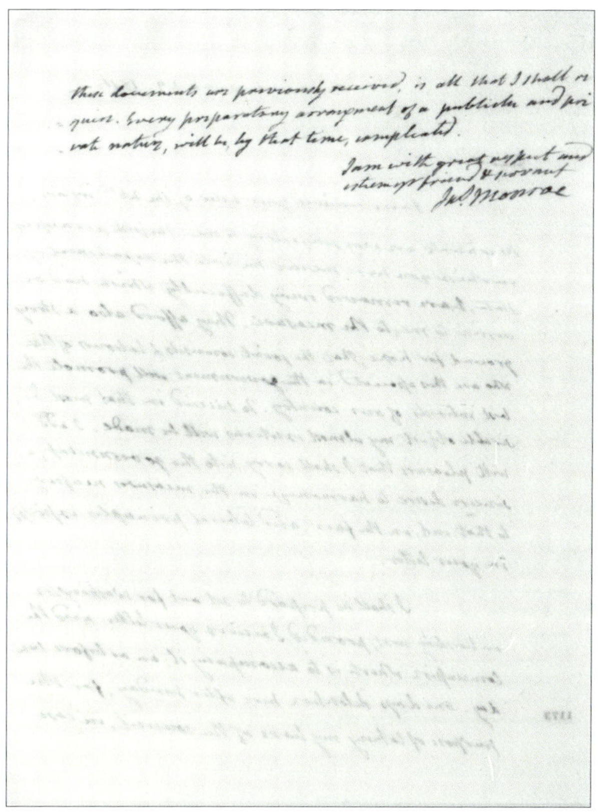

these documents are previously received, is all that I shall require. Every preparatory arrangement of a publick and private nature, will be, by that time, compleated.

I am with great respect and esteem your friend & servant

Jas. Monroe

Library of Congress, Manuscript Division, Madison Papers

Monroe's old friend George Clinton of New York was vice president during Madison's first term. He died in office in April 1812.

New York Historical Society

country, making it difficult for Madison to marshal resources. American strategy for fighting the war was also a problem. The Madison administration thought that the United States could score several quick victories in an invasion of Canada and thereby force concessions from Great Britain. Canadian resistance blocked the invasion, which resulted in a stalemate along the border that continued until the end of the war. The American navy won a number of impressive victories early in the war, but the navy was too small to conduct a sustained sea war. The United States defeated the Indian nations allied with Great Britain, but it made no permanent gains against the British.

Much of the problem resulted from poor leadership in Washington. William Eustis, Madison's first secretary of war, became completely overwhelmed by the task of managing the war and resigned in December 1812. Monroe served for several weeks as secretary ad interim until John Armstrong was appointed to the post in February 1813. Armstrong enjoyed Madison's trust, but he was unable to bring about a vigorous prosecution of the war. Both Monroe and Secretary of the Treasury Albert Gallatin were increasingly dissatisfied with the lackluster conduct of the war, and Monroe even contemplated resigning from the cabinet. By the summer of 1814 the war had lost so much

Another old friend, Elbridge Gerry of Massachusetts, was Madison's vice president during his second term. He too died in office, in November 1814. Fogg Art Museum, Harvard

Albert Gallatin, who served as secretary of treasury under both Jefferson and Madison, was the dominant member of Madison's cabinet at the time Monroe joined it. Gallatin served as minister to France during Monroe's administration. National Portrait Gallery, Washington

popular support that the government had trouble commanding the credit necessary to purchase military supplies. Not only was the United States losing the war, it was close to bankruptcy.

Then, in August 1814, the United States profited from the most unusual circumstance—the British captured the nation's capital. Monroe had warned throughout the war that Washington was vulnerable to attack, but neither Armstrong nor Madison saw any threat. When a British column began to march towards the city in August 1814 Monroe, frustrated by the inaction in Washington and eager for military duty, took to the field with a troop of cavalry and scouted the enemy's advance. The Americans threw together a makeshift army near the town of Bladensburg, Maryland, but it was inadequate to stop the British. There was no clear chain of command among the disparate units brought together at Bladensburg; Monroe added to the confusion by repositioning some the troops and not informing other officers. The British easily broke the American line and marched into Washington, which had been abandoned by the government and what was left of the army. They burned the Capitol, the President's House, several other buildings, and then withdrew. Madison dismissed Armstrong as secretary of war and named Monroe in his place. Monroe served concurrently as secretary of state and secretary of war from September 1814 to March 1815.

Ironically, the burning of Washington galvanized the war effort. Americans all along the Atlantic coast, fearful that the British would attack and burn other cities, began to pour money into the defense effort. Monroe, with his great energy and administrative skills, brought new order to the army as he began to organize and supply it for the upcoming summer campaign. The war effort received a boost on the battlefield as well. After leaving Washington, the British launched an attack on Baltimore that was repulsed, giving the Americans a much needed victory. These efforts were crowned by Andrew Jackson's stunning defeat of the British at New Orleans in January 1815.

Efforts to negotiate a peace began almost as soon as the war started. The British, in an about-face caused by increasing economic problems, relaxed their restrictions on

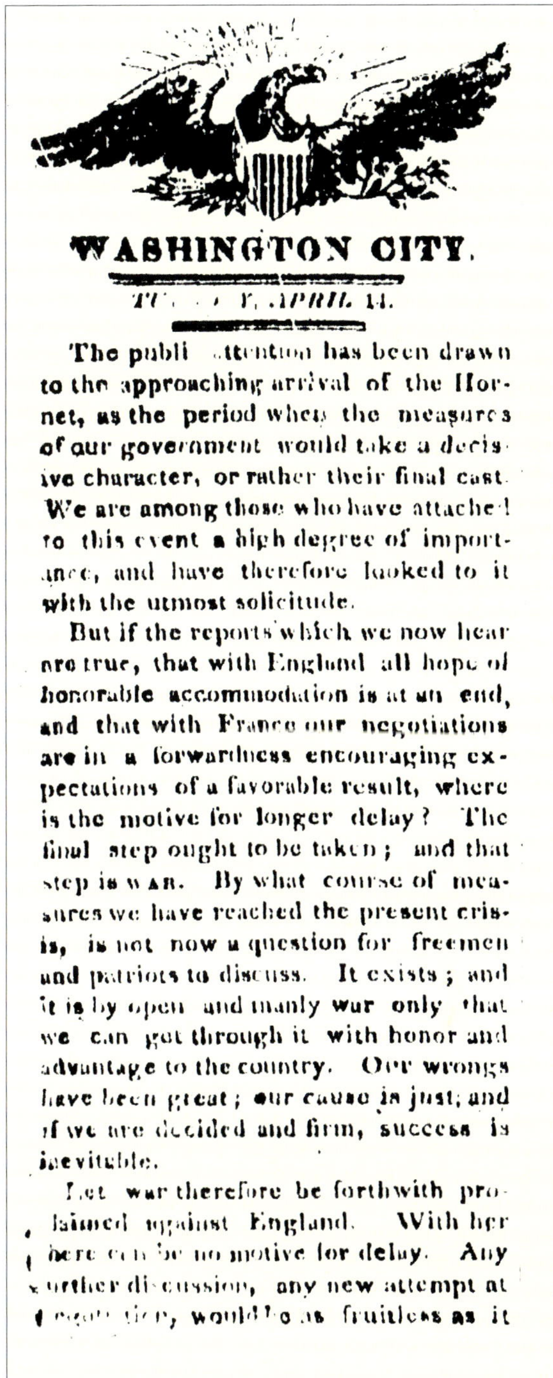

WASHINGTON CITY.

TUESDAY, APRIL 14.

The public attention has been drawn to the approaching arrival of the Hornet, as the period when the measures of our government would take a decisive character, or rather their final cast. We are among those who have attached to this event a high degree of importance, and have therefore looked to it with the utmost solicitude.

But if the reports which we now hear are true, that with England all hope of honorable accommodation is at an end, and that with France our negotiations are in a forwardness encouraging expectations of a favorable result, where is the motive for longer delay? The final step ought to be taken; and that step is WAR. By what course of measures we have reached the present crisis, is not now a question for freemen and patriots to discuss. It exists; and it is by open and manly war only that we can get through it with honor and advantage to the country. Our wrongs have been great; our cause is just; and if we are decided and firm, success is inevitable.

Let war therefore be forthwith proclaimed against England. With her there can be no motive for delay. Any further discussion, any new attempt at negotiation, would be as fruitless as it

Having failed to attain a negotiated settlement, Monroe concluded that war was inevitable and wrote a series of newspaper essays presenting the administration's case for declaring war.

WASHINGTON NATIONAL INTELLIGENCER, 14 APRIL 1812

John Armstrong

by Rembrandt Peale,
Independence National Historical Park

William Eustis

by Walter Brackett,
U. S. Center of Military History, Washington

WEARING TWO HATS

William Eustis was Madison's first secretary of war. He resigned in early December 1812, and Monroe became acting secretary of war, filling the position until early February 1813 when John Armstrong took over the office. Armstrong served until the disastrous attack on Washington at the end of August 1814. Monroe then returned to the war office, serving concurrently as secretary of war and secretary of state, executing these dual responsibilities until March 1815.

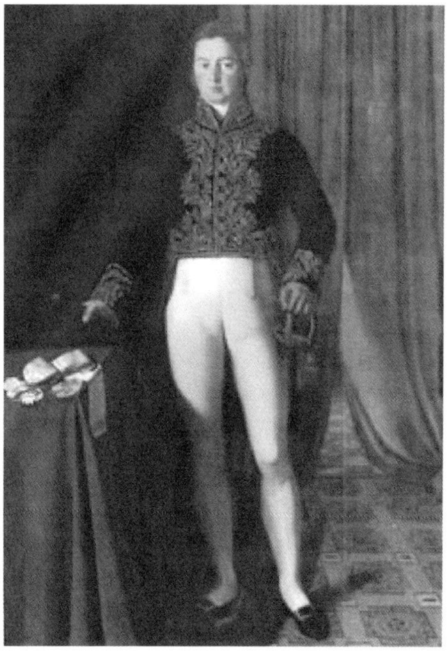

Monroe had hoped to obtain a negotiated settlement with Great Britain, but relations between the two countries had deteriorated to an irreversible point by the time Monroe became secretary of state. His efforts to reach an agreement with British minister Augustus Foster proved to be in vain.

Government Art Collection of Great Britain

American shipping on almost the same day that the United States declared war. Both sides sensing a possibility for peace proposed conditional armistices, but neither side found the proposed terms acceptable. These overtures were followed by an offer from Czar Alexander of Russia to mediate peace talks between the two countries. The United States, seeing the offer as an advantageous one, accepted immediately. The British, likewise sensing that mediation would favor the United States, countered with an offer of direct negotiations. The United States accepted and the treaty commissioners met in Ghent, Belgium in August 1814. Both sides were weary of war, and the negotiations progressed from demands for the redress of grievances to simply agreeing to stop fighting. The commissioners signed a treaty of peace on December 24, 1814.

The United States was greatly relieved by the return of peace. The repulse of the British at Baltimore and Jackson's victory at New Orleans at the end of the war gave the impression that the United States had been able to hold its own against the greatest power in Europe. But Madison and Monroe knew how tenuous the situation had been. Both recognized a need to strengthen the nation's defenses and worked to this end during the last two years of Madison's administration. As secretary of war Monroe drafted a detailed plan for the reorganization of the army. As secretary of state he oversaw the re-establishment of the diplomatic and consular corps, which had been badly disrupted by the years of commercial and actual warfare. He also oversaw the writing of new treaties with foreign nations, and negotiated the most important of these himself. Both the United States and Great Britain were concerned that tension between American and British forces along the Canadian border would lead to an unintentional renewal of the war. Monroe suggested to Charles Bagot, the British minister to the United States, that a sure way to avoid this was for both nations to disarm along the border. Monroe and Bagot negotiated such a treaty in the closing months of the Madison administration, but it was not approved by Great Britain until after Monroe had become president. Known as the Rush-Bagot Agreement (named for Richard Rush, the acting secretary of state in the opening months of Monroe's presidency, who signed it), the treaty set strict limitations on armaments on the Great Lakes.

Charles Bagot was the British minister to the United States 1816–1819. He and Monroe negotiated a treaty in 1816 for disarmament on the Great Lakes. Known as the Rush-Bagot Agreement, it was signed by Acting Secretary of State Richard Rush in April 1817 after Monroe had become president.

National Portrait Gallery, London

Library of Congress, Prints and Photographs Division

THE WAR AT SEA

The American navy scored some impressive victories early in the war, one of the most famous being the *United States* over the *Macedonian* (above). The American navy was small, however, and was supplemented by privateers, such as *The America* (at right), which sailed out of Salem, Massachusetts. These privateers carried commissions and instructions issued by Monroe as secretary of state (facing page).

Edgar Stanton Maclay, *A History of American Privateers*

To Captain Robert Evans *commander of the private armed* Schooner *called the* Orlando.

INSTRUCTIONS

FOR THE PRIVATE ARMED VESSELS OF THE UNITED STATES.

1. THE tenor of your commission under the act of Congress, entitled "An act concerning letters of marque, prizes, and prize goods," a copy of which is hereto annexed, will be kept constantly in your view. The high seas, referred to in your commission, you will understand, generally, to extend to low water mark; but with the exception of the space within one league, or three miles, from the shore of countries at peace both with Great Britain and with the United States. You may nevertheless execute your commission within that distance of the shore of a nation at war with Great Britain, and even on the waters within the jurisdiction of such nation, if permitted so to do.

2. You are to pay the strictest regard to the rights of neutral powers, and the usages of civilized nations; and in all your proceedings towards neutral vessels, you are to give them as little molestation or interruption as will consist with the right of ascertaining their neutral character, and of detaining and bringing them in for regular adjudication, in the proper cases. You are particularly to avoid even the appearance of using force or seduction, with a view to deprive such vessels of their crews, or of their passengers, other than persons in the military service of the enemy.

3. Towards enemy vessels and their crews, you are to proceed, in exercising the rights of war, with all the justice and humanity which characterize the nation of which you are members.

4. The master and one or more of the principal persons belonging to captured vessels, are to be sent, as soon after the capture as may be, to the judge or judges of the proper court in the United States, to be examined upon oath, touching the interest or property of the captured vessel and her lading: and at the same time are to be delivered to the judge or judges, all passes, charter parties, bills of lading, invoices, letters and other documents and writings found on board; the said papers to be proved by the affidavit of the commander of the capturing vessel, or some other person present at the capture, to be produced as they were received, without fraud, addition, subduction or embezzlement.

By command of the President of the United States of America.

Jas Monroe Secretary of State.

Chapin Library, Williams College, Williamstown, MA

Library of Congress, Prints and Photographs Division

THE SACK OF WASHINGTON

The British easily brushed aside the disorganized American force gathered at Bladensburg, Maryland to block the British advance on Washington. Once in the city the British burned the Capitol, the President's House, and several other buildings. Monroe, who had warned of an attack on Washington, tried to take a hand in the defense of the city and unwisely repositioned some troops at Bladensburg. He was the first government official to return to Washington; fearful that the British might make a second attack, he organized the few troops he could find for the defense of the city.

Artillery battery manned by U. S. Marines fighting at Bladensburg.

Art Collection, National Museum of the Marine Corps, Triangle, VA

Burned shells of the President's House, above, and the Capitol, below.

LIBRARY OF CONGRESS, PRINTS AND PHOTOGRAPHS DIVISION

After leaving Washington the British attacked Baltimore. American forces there repulsed both a land attack on the city and a naval assault on Fort McHenry. Monroe, as the new secretary of war, coordinated the movement of troops to Baltimore.

MARYLAND HISTORICAL SOCIETY

When Monroe learned that a British expedition was headed for New Orleans, he sent troops and supplies to the city and instructed Andrew Jackson to take command. Jackson's great victory at New Orleans made him a national hero and helped create the illusion that the United States had won the war. LIBRARY OF CONGRESS, PRINTS AND PHOTOGRAPHS DIVISION

Monroe, as secretary of state, conveyed President Madison's instructions to the American commissioners negotiating a peace treaty at Ghent, Belgium. The treaty was signed at Ghent on December 24, 1814, and ratified at Washington on February 17, 1815. NATIONAL LIBRARY OF CANADA, OTTAWA

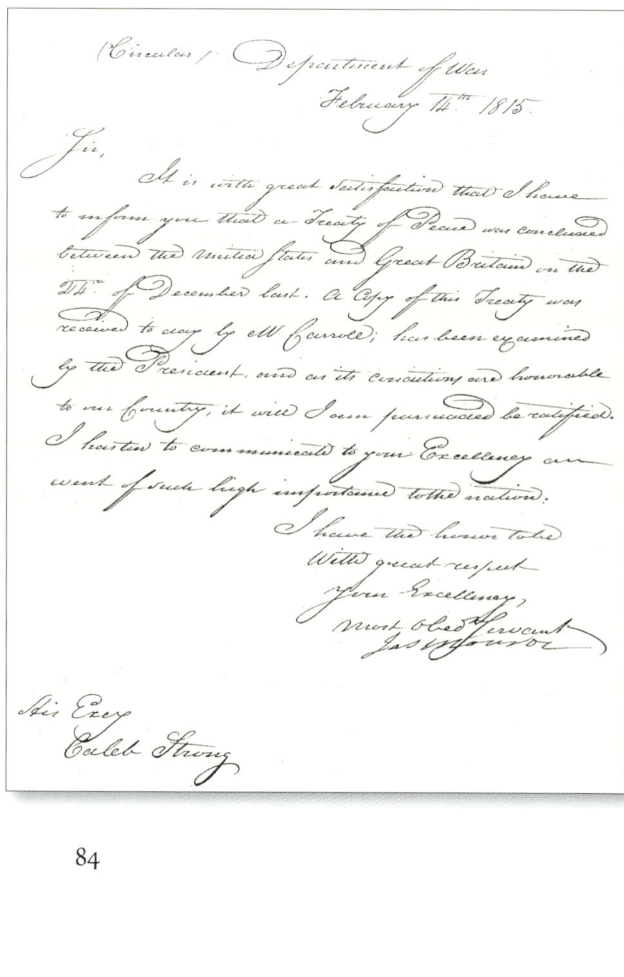

(Circular) Department of War
February 14th 1815.

Sir,

It is with great satisfaction that I have to inform you that a Treaty of Peace was concluded between the United States and Great Britain on the 24th of December last. A Copy of this Treaty was received to day by Mr Carroll; has been examined by the President, and as its conditions are honorable to our Country, it will I am persuaded be ratified. I hasten to communicate to your Excellency an event of such high importance to the nation.

I have the honor to be
With great respect
Your Excellency,
most obed. Servant
Jas Monroe

His Excy
Caleb Strong

Monroe wrote to the governors of the states as soon as the treaty arrived in Washington and informed them of the peace.

MASSACHUSETTS STATE ARCHIVES, BOSTON

James Monroe

OAK HILL

James Monroe and his uncle, Joseph Jones, purchased a 2,000 acre tract of land in Loudoun County, Virginia in 1794. Monroe inherited Jones's portion of the land in 1808 and thus became owner of the entire tract. Monroe, not needing two large farms in Virginia, tried to sell the Loudoun County property but was unsuccessful. When Monroe became secretary of state he found it to be much easier to travel to Loudoun than to Albemarle from Washington. There was a small two-story house on the farm (which the Monroes named Oak Hill) that the Monroes used, but as they began to spend more time there, they decided to build a larger house. Jefferson helped with the design, and architect James Hoban supervised the construction, which began in 1818. The Monroes spent their summers away from Washington, and divided their time between the two farms. Oak Hill was more convenient to Washington (it was only a few hours ride from the city), and the new house was more comfortable, but the Monroes had grown attached to Highland and spent a considerable amount of time there. Monroe decided after he left the presidency that he had to sell one of his farms. He kept Oak Hill, and it served as the family residence from 1826 until 1831. Monroe left Oak Hill to his daughter Maria Gouverneur (he had given his other daughter, Eliza Hay, a farm when she married). The Gouverneurs owned Oak Hill until after Maria's death in 1850, when it was sold out of the family. It remains a private home.

Oak Hill, Monroe's home in Loudoun County, Virginia. Monroe acquired full title to this property in 1808. Prior to the construction of the large house in 1819, he and his family used the smaller house shown on the left. Library of Virginia

Above: This exhibit at the James Monroe Museum in Fredericksburg of furniture and artifacts owned by the Monroes is arranged to represent the dining room at Oak Hill.

James Monroe Museum

Left: This old photograph of the entry hall at Oak Hill shows furniture owned by the Monroes.

James Monroe Museum

Monroe sent his wheat to be ground at the Aldie Mill, which had been built and was owned by his neighbor and friend Charles Fenton Mercer.

VIRGINIA DEPARTMENT OF HISTORIC RESOURCES

Plowing. BENJAMIN BUTTERWORTH, *THE GROWTH OF INDUSTRIAL ART*

"We began sowing wheat today. . . . It is rolled in lime, & will be plaistered when it comes up. It is previously soaked in salt & water 12 hours. This is done to protect it against the smut; it succeeded whenever it was tried in this neighborhood last year."

—MONROE TO AN UNKNOWN CORRESPONDENT, 14 APRIL 1818

Reaping. BENJAMIN BUTTERWORTH, *THE GROWTH OF INDUSTRIAL ART*

James Monroe by John Vanderlyn, 1816. This portrait was originally owned by James Madison. A copy owned by Monroe is in the National Portrait Gallery in Washington. Colonial Williamsburg Foundation

This portrait of Elizabeth Monroe by Frances Maury Burke was painted in the early 20th century and copied the original by John Vanderlyn, which was painted in 1816. The original, which is privately owned, is on display in the Blue Room at the White House.

James Monroe Museum

"Vanderlyn the painter is at present in town, he has taken excellent likenesses of Mr. Madison, Mr. Crowninshield, Mrs. Monroe, Mrs. Hay and others."

—Ellen Randolph Coolidge to Martha Jefferson Randolph, 17 February 1816

Pencil sketch of James Monroe by John Vanderlyn.

Special Collections, Swem Library, College of William and Mary

James Monroe

PRESIDENT OF THE UNITED STATES

JAMES MONROE was the Republican nominee for president in 1816. Some Republicans, reluctant to elect another Virginian, backed William H. Crawford of Georgia, the secretary of the treasury in Madison's cabinet. National support for Monroe was overwhelming, however, and he became his party's candidate. Senator Rufus King was the Federalist candidate. Monroe won easily, garnering 183 electoral votes to King's thirty-four. Monroe was inaugurated as the fifth president of the United States on March 4, 1817. Daniel D. Tompkins of New York became vice president.

James Monroe by Rembrandt Peale, ca. 1824.

JAMES MONROE MUSEUM

A first priority for Monroe as president was the strengthening of the nation's defenses. Congress had made provision for the construction and improvement of coastal fortifications. Monroe, wanting to gain first-hand information on the state of the forts, set out on a tour of inspection in June 1817. He inspected military installations from Baltimore north to Maine and along the Canadian border, and returned home through Ohio, Pennsylvania, and Maryland. His fourteen-week journey became a grand national celebration, for Monroe was the first president since Washington to make a tour of the country. People all along the route, thrilled

James Monroe by Margaret French Cresson, 1929.

James Monroe Museum

James Monroe by Harmon MacNeil.

Hall of Fame of Great Americans,
Bronx College, New York

at the opportunity of seeing the president, came out by the thousands and welcomed Monroe with parades, speeches, dinners, balls, and festivities of all sorts. In 1819 he traveled down the coast from Washington to Savannah and then inland to Tennessee, Kentucky, and Indiana. His reception in the south was as grand as it had been in the north.

When Monroe returned to Washington from his northern tour in September 1817 he and his family moved into the newly restored White House. As its first occupant since the fire in 1814 Monroe was responsible for furnishing the house. Monroe believed that the president's home should be furnished in a fashion that would reflect the rising grandeur of the United States. He used some of his own furniture that he had purchased in Europe and ordered additional items from France and from American furniture makers. Most of the Monroe items were replaced when later presidents brought in new furniture, but some are still in use at the White House, most notably in the Blue Room.

Another pressing priority for Monroe was the acquisition of Florida. The United States had always considered the Spanish possessions on its southern border as a threat. The United States wanted very much to acquire this territory, and Jefferson had sent Monroe to Spain in 1805 to try to negotiate an arrangement for its purchase. The peninsula was as critical to the defense

James Monroe, painted by Gilbert Stuart in Boston in 1817.

National Gallery of Art, Washington

James Monroe by Charles Bird King, 1817. Loudoun County Court House, Leesburg, VA

James Monroe by Attilio Piccirilli, 1930. Virginia State Capitol, Richmond and Ash Lawn-Highland

of Spanish territory as it was to the United States, and Spain had no desire to sell it. By 1817 Florida had become problematic. Spain's control of the area was tenuous, and hostile Indians, smugglers, and runaway slaves all used it as a refuge. In 1817 a group of South American revolutionaries attempted to capture Florida to use as a base to attack Cuba. The expedition fell apart, and the United States army occupied the region north of St. Augustine to prevent further incursions. The following year General Andrew Jackson invaded Florida while pursuing hostile Indians. This growing pressure persuaded Spain to open negotiations, and in 1819 it agreed to cede Florida to the United States. This treaty, negotiated by Secretary of State John Quincy Adams, also contained provisions for setting the boundary between Spanish and American territory west of the Mississippi. Adams also negotiated treaties with Great Britain and Russia that defined the American border on the north and recognized American claims in the Pacific Northwest. Altogether, these three treaties defined the bounds of the United States and secured the nation's claims to territory on the Pacific coast.

The 1819 treaty with Spain resolved one longstanding problem for the United States, but two severe crises arose in that same year. The first was an economic depression, known as the Panic of 1819. The panic caused severe hardship, but the national economy was strong enough to weather the storm, and prosperity returned in several years. A more dangerous crisis materialized that year when Missouri applied for admittance to the union as a state. A group of northern congressmen, hoping to block the spread of slavery, attached an amendment to the statehood bill that made a ban on slavery in the new state a condition for admittance. Missouri objected to this amendment, as did the congressmen from the slave states, who threatened disunion over the issue. President Monroe thought the legislation to be unconstitutional, since it placed a restriction on one state that did not apply to others, and said he would veto it. He was more concerned, however, by the talk of disunion. When moderates in Congress began to work out a compromise, Monroe did all he could to support it. It was considered improper at the time for the president to openly involve himself in legislative matters, so Monroe worked quietly to help secure passage of the compromise. He was satisfied with the terms of the compromise—which allowed slavery in Missouri but banned it in most of the territory acquired in the Louisiana Purchase—and signed the legislation. Monroe, afraid that internal tensions would divide the union (and destroy the nation), was greatly relieved by the acceptance of the compromise.

Monroe was re-elected to a second term as president in 1820 without opposition. There were many men with presidential aspirations, but they all knew that Monroe would easily win, so they chose not to waste any political capital in a futile effort. He received every electoral vote except one. He took the oath of office at the newly restored Capitol on March 4, 1821.

Monroe was never an outspoken opponent of slavery, but by the time he became president he had come to favor its elimination. He did not believe that blacks could be integrated into American society and therefore espoused a plan of compensated emancipation and the colonization of the freed slaves outside the United States. He was a strong supporter of the American Colonization Society, and when that organization established a colony for freed blacks in 1821 in what is now Liberia they named the settlement Monrovia in his honor. As president he could, of course, do nothing directly to end slavery. He could and did, however, attack the slave trade. He ordered the navy to destroy several smuggling enclaves that served as conduits for bringing slaves illegally into the United States, he espoused an international treaty to outlaw the slave trade, and when Congress declared the slave trade to be an act of piracy in 1820 he ordered the navy squadrons in the Atlantic and the Caribbean to intercept any ships suspected of engaging in the trade.

In 1822 the United States became the first nation to recognize the independence of the new nations of Latin America. Revolutions erupted throughout Spain's

William H. Crawford

Charles Bird King,
Redwood Library and Athenaeum,
Newport, RI

HIS RIVALS

Monroe's chief rival for the presidency in 1816 was William H. Crawford of Georgia. Crawford was the secretary of the treasury in Madison's cabinet, a position he continued to hold during Monroe's two terms.

Senator Rufus King of New York was the Federalist candidate for president in 1816. King won only thirty-four electoral votes to Monroe's 183 and carried only Massachusetts, Connecticut, and Delaware.

Rufus King

Gilbert Stuart, National Portrait
Gallery, Washington

American empire beginning in 1808. Their fortunes waxed and waned over the next fourteen years until it became clear that the revolutionary governments had secured their independence. These revolutions had received widespread support in the United States. The Madison and Monroe administrations shared this sentiment but, wary of being drawn into another war, adhered to a policy of neutrality. Advocates of the revolutionaries, led by Henry Clay, the powerful speaker of the House of Representatives, urged Monroe as soon as he became president to express American support for the Spanish Americans by recognizing their independence. Monroe refused to be drawn into the conflict. He acted quickly, however, as soon as the revolutionaries had demonstrated that they had established their independence. In 1822 he extended recognition to Mexico and Gran Colombia (present day Colombia, Venezuela, and Ecuador); in 1823 he recognized Chile and Argentina; in 1824, Brazil and the Federation of Central American States (Costa Rica, Panama, and Nicaragua).

Monroe took his oath of office as president March 4, 1817, on the front balcony of what is know as the "old brick capitol." This building, located on the present site of the U. S. Supreme Court, was constructed in 1815 as a temporary home for Congress while the Capitol was being rebuilt.

PAINTING BY ALLYN COX, U. S. CONGRESS

Great Britain soon followed suit, but Spain and its allies refused to acknowledge the independence of these colonies. Indeed, Spain still harbored hopes of reasserting control over the region. When Spain and its allies began to talk of sending an expedition to South America to try to suppress the revolutions British prime minister George Canning suggested that the United States unite with Great Britain to oppose the move. Monroe gave careful consideration to the proposal but decided that it would be better for the United States to make a stand on its own. In his annual message to Congress of December 2, 1823, he pronounced what is now known as the Monroe Doctrine. Monroe warned the European nations that any attempt to suppress the new governments would be considered as a "manifestation of an unfriendly disposition toward the United States." He also announced that the Americas were now closed to any new colonization efforts. At the same time he reaffirmed the traditional American policy of American neutrality in European affairs. Monroe's challenge was never put to the test, for Great Britain had extracted a pledge from France that it would not aid Spain in any attempt to regain its colonies, a promise that put an end to the proposed expedition. Even so, Monroe's declaration of an American sphere of interest in the Western Hemisphere became a cornerstone of American foreign policy for years to come.

Monroe's retirement from the presidency led to a mad scramble to succeed him. A host of candidates coveted the office, and without two viable parties to contest the elections (the Federalists having collapsed as a national party) four candidates battled for the position: Secretary of State John Quincy Adams, Secretary of the Treasury William H. Crawford, Henry Clay, the Speaker of the House of Representatives, and General Andrew Jackson. Secretary of War John C. Calhoun withdrew his candidacy for president and became a candidate for vice president. Monroe sought to avoid any involvement in the election to the extent of eschewing any contact with the candidates outside of their official duties. Monroe was able to retain his good humor, despite having most everyone about him running for president, telling Attorney General William Wirt that he would be glad of a visit from him at Oak Hill: "It will give me pleasure to see you here," he wrote, " you not being a candidate for a certain office." No one candidate received the necessary majority, and the election went to the House of Representatives, which chose John Quincy Adams. Monroe attended Adams's inauguration on March 4, 1825 and then went home.

Monroe and Chief Justice John Marshall re-established their friendship while Monroe was serving as secretary of state. Monroe wrote to Marshall on March 1, 1817, asking him to administer the oath of office at his inauguration.

PORTRAIT BY HENRY INMAN
LIBRARY OF VIRGINIA, RICHMOND

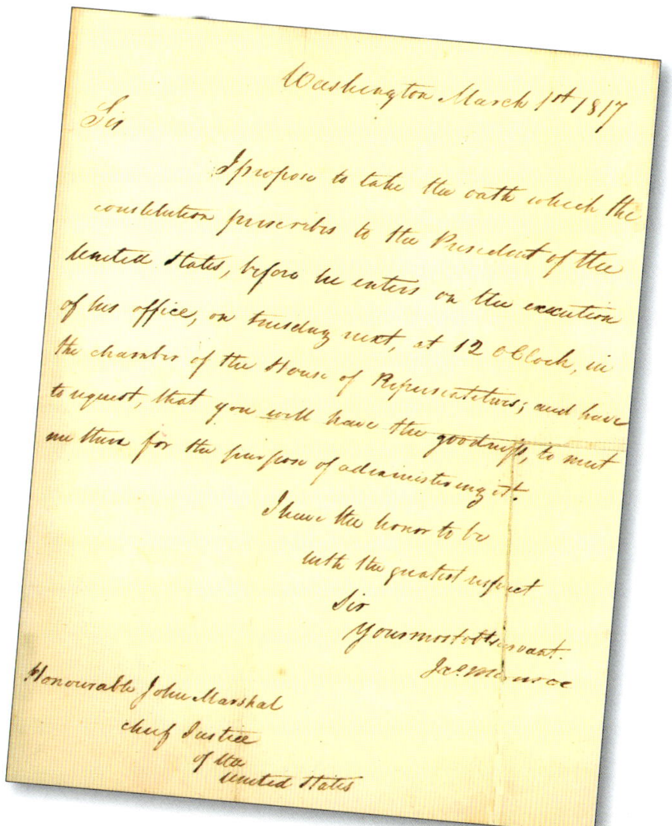

Washington March 1st 1817

Sir

I propose to take the oath which the constitution prescribes to the President of the united states, before he enters on the execution of his office, on tuesday next, at 12 o'Clock, in the chamber of the House of Representatives; and have to request, that you will have the goodness, to meet me there for the purpose of administering it.

I have the honor to be
with the greatest respect
Sir
Your most obt servant.
Jas Monroe

Honourable John Marshal
chief Justice
of the
united states

MARSHALL PAPERS, SWEM LIBRARY,
THE COLLEGE OF WILLIAM AND MARY

HIS APPOINTMENTS

Monroe chose the highly able John C. Calhoun of South Carolina to head the War Department. He selected John Quincy Adams, the only man in the country with diplomatic experience to match his own, to serve as secretary of state. And Daniel D. Tompkins, the former governor of New York, served as Monroe's vice president.

John C. Calhoun

Charles Bird King,
Redwood Library and Athenaeum

John Quincy Adams

Gilbert Stuart, Harvard University Art Gallery, Cambridge, MA

Daniel D. Tompkins

Historical Society of the Courts of the State of New York,
White Plains, NY

William Wirt

Charles Bird King, Redwood Library and Athenaeum

Richard Rush

Engraving by Joseph Ives Pease, Smithsonian Institution Archives, Washington

HIS FRIENDS

Monroe frequently went riding or walking with Attorney General William Wirt, who was, perhaps, his closest friend among the members of the cabinet.

Monroe's good friend Richard Rush had been attorney general in Madison's cabinet. He continued in that capacity under Monroe until October 1817, when William Wirt assumed the duties. Rush also served as secretary of state ad interim until John Quincy Adams arrived from England in September 1817. Monroe then appointed Rush as minister to Great Britain.

"As the elevated ground, which [Monroe] already holds, has been gained merely by the dint of application; as every new step which he mounts becomes a mean of increasing his powers still further, by opening a wider horizon to his view, and thus stimulating his enterprise afresh, reinvigorating his habits, multiplying the materials and extending the range of his knowledge; it would be matter of no surprise to me, if, before his death, the world should see him at the head of the American administration."

—William Wirt, *The Letters of a British Spy*, 1803

Samuel Southard

A. S. Conrad, U. S. Navy Art Collection

HIS NAVY SECRETARIES

Benjamin Crowninshield, who was secretary of the navy under Madison, continued in that office until the end of 1818, when he resigned. Smith Thompson of New York replaced him and held the post until September 1823 when Monroe appointed him to the Supreme Court (Monroe's only appointment to the court). He was succeeded by Samuel Southard of New Jersey.

Smith Thompson

Asher B. Durand
U. S. Supreme Court

Benjamin Crowninshield

U. D. Tenney
U. S. Navy Art Collection, Washington, DC

HIS 1817 TOUR

Monroe made three tours of the country during his presidency: in 1817 he toured the northern states, in 1818 he made a cruise around Chesapeake Bay, and in 1819 he traveled through the southern states.

Daniel Preston, The Papers of James Monroe, Volume 1: The Presidential Tours of James Monroe
Maps by Arrow Graphics

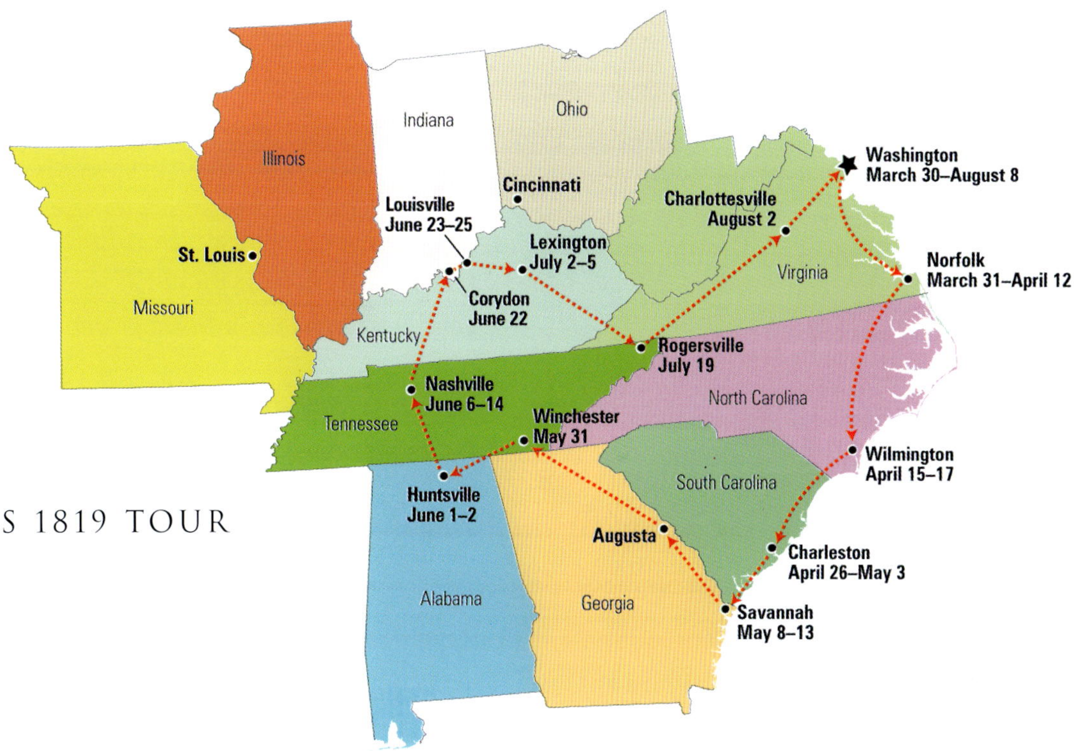

HIS 1819 TOUR

During his tours Monroe inspected military installations along the Atlantic coast and the Canadian border, including Fort Niagara.

BENJAMIN LOSSING, *PICTORIAL FIELD-BOOK OF THE WAR OF 1812*

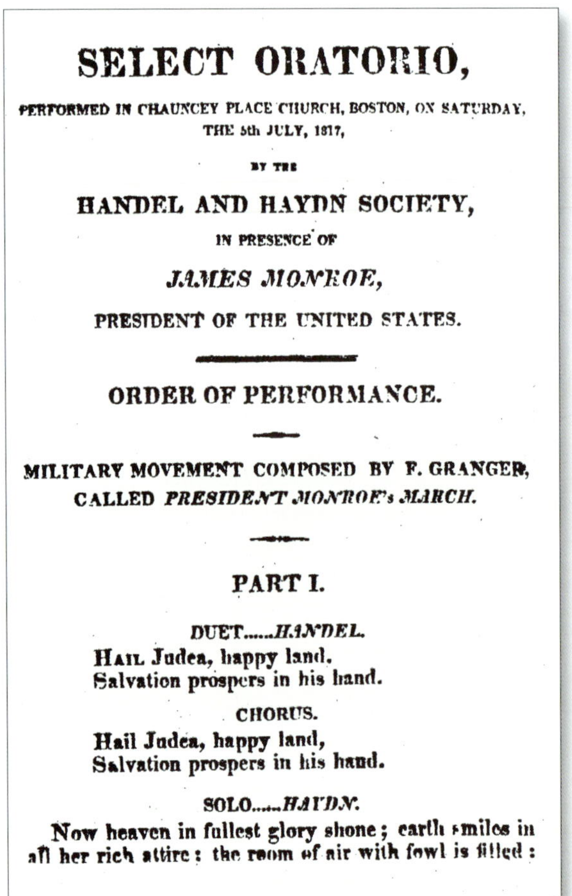

SELECT ORATORIO,

PERFORMED IN CHAUNCEY PLACE CHURCH, BOSTON, ON SATURDAY, THE 5th JULY, 1817,

BY THE

HANDEL AND HAYDN SOCIETY,

IN PRESENCE OF

JAMES MONROE,

PRESIDENT OF THE UNITED STATES.

ORDER OF PERFORMANCE.

MILITARY MOVEMENT COMPOSED BY F. GRANGER, CALLED *PRESIDENT MONROE's MARCH.*

PART I.

DUET.....*HANDEL.*

HAIL Judea, happy land.
Salvation prospers in his hand.

CHORUS.

Hail Judea, happy land,
Salvation prospers in his hand.

SOLO.....*HAYDN.*

Now heaven in fullest glory shone; earth smiles in all her rich attire: the room of air with fowl is filled:

EARLY AMERICAN IMPRINTS

NEWBERRY LIBRARY, CHICAGO, IL

Monroe's tours became great celebratory events, with parades, receptions, dinners, balls, and even breakfasts given in his honor, and with songs and poems written to mark the occasion.

RICHMOND (VA) ENQUIRER, 11 MAY 1819

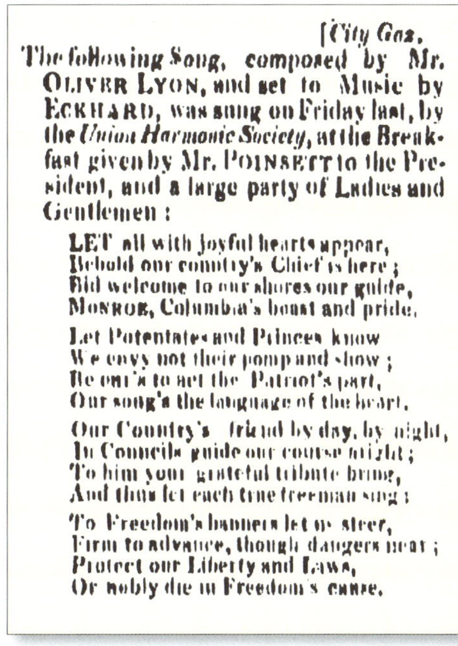

[City Gaz.

The following Song, composed by Mr. OLIVER LYON, and set to Music by ECKHARD, was sung on Friday last, by the *Union Harmonic Society*, at the Breakfast given by Mr. POINSETT to the President, and a large party of Ladies and Gentlemen:

LET all with joyful hearts appear,
Behold our country's Chief is here;
Bid welcome to our shores our guide,
MONROE, Columbia's boast and pride.

Let Potentates and Princes know
We envy not their pomp and show;
Be our's to act the Patriot's part,
Our song's the language of the heart.

Our Country's friend by day, by night,
In Councils guide our course aright;
To him your grateful tribute bring,
And thus let each true freeman sing:

To Freedom's banners let us steer,
Firm to advance, though dangers near;
Protect our Liberty and Laws,
Or nobly die in Freedom's cause.

A large and enthusiastic crowd greeted Monroe on his return to Washington in September 1817. He is shown here outside the White House receiving congratulations of the citizens of the city. (JAMES MONROE MUSEUM) *"On his arrival at his residence, the President dismounted and was received by a number of his fellow citizens, who waited his arrival. In behalf of the citizens of Washington who had formed a part of the cavalcade, General J. P. Van Ness delivered to the president a verbal salutation."* —WASHINGTON NATIONAL INTELLIGENCER, 19 SEPTEMBER 1817

A view of the White House, painted in the mid 1820s by Anthony St. John Baker. The Capitol is in the distance, on the right.

Huntington Library, San Marino, CA

The U. S. Capitol in 1824.

Library of Congress, Prints and Photographs Division

The city of Charleston commissioned Samuel F. B. Morse (later famous for inventing the telegraph) to paint a portrait of Monroe. It now hangs in the Charleston city hall.

City of Charleston, SC

The Elliptical Salon exhibit at the Monroe Museum, arranged to represent a room in the Monroe White House.

James Monroe Museum

A view of the Blue Room at the White House, showing furniture and ornaments acquired by Monroe. Portraits of James and Elizabeth Monroe hang on the wall.

The White House

A view of the newly restored White House, painted in 1821 by the Baroness Hyde de Neuville, the wife of the French minister to the United States. The brick buildings were the offices of the departments of government.

New York Public Library, Stokes Collection

TROUBLE WITH SPAIN

When the war in Europe ended in 1815 Spain directed its attention to its rebellious colonies and within a year had suppressed the revolution in many parts of its American empire. Many revolutionary leaders fled to the United States where they made preparations to strike back at the Spanish. Gregor MacGregor, a British soldier in the service of Colombia, organized an expedition in New York to invade Spanish Florida. McGregor captured Amelia Island, a Spanish outpost on the Florida-Georgia border in August 1817. He was unable to move forward from there, and his expedition unraveled. Monroe had waited to see the results of MacGregor's undertaking, and when it collapsed he sent the navy to occupy Amelia Island and secure the border against future disorder.

Gregor MacGregor

PORTRAIT OF MACGREGOR IS FROM AN ENGRAVING BY SAMUEL W. REYNOLDS IN THE NATIONAL PORTRAIT GALLERY, LONDON

Andrew Jackson precipitated a crisis with Spain when he captured two Spanish posts in Florida while pursuing marauding Indians.

PORTRAIT BY RALPH EARL, NATIONAL PORTRAIT GALLERY, WASHINGTON

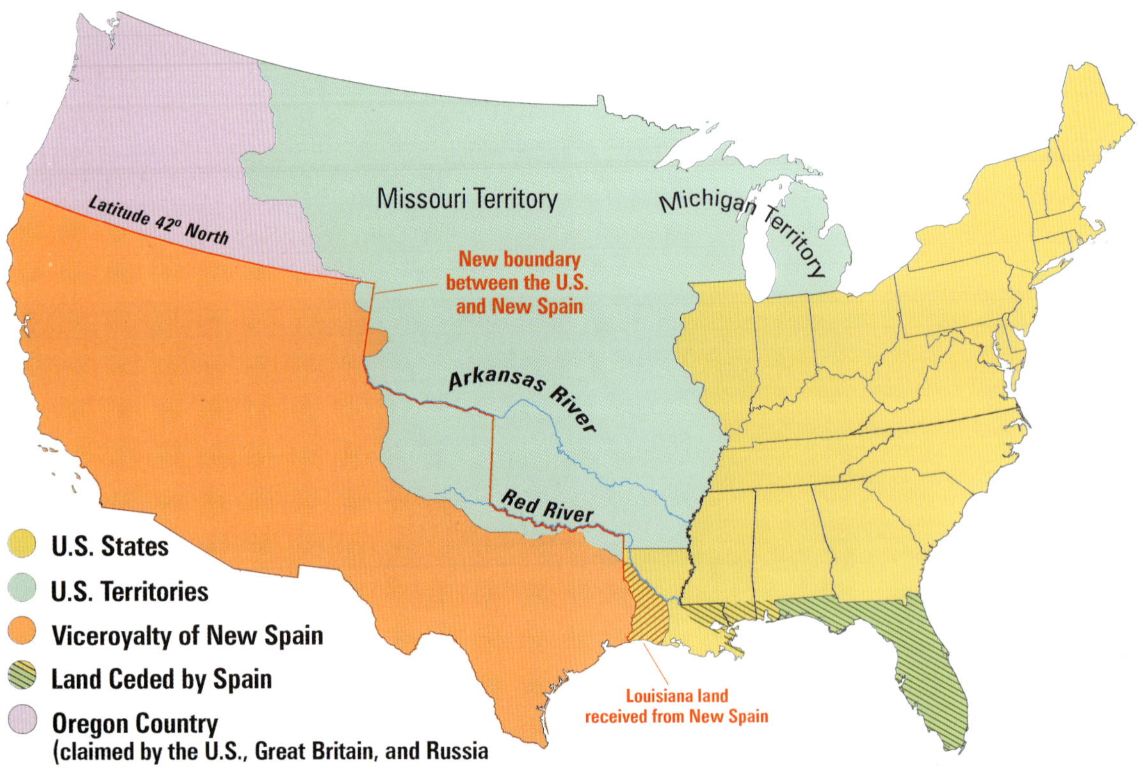

Secretary of State John Quincy Adams negotiated a treaty in 1819 with Luis de Onis, the Spanish minister to the United States, that ceded Florida to the United States and set the border between American and Spanish territory west of the Mississippi. MAP BY ARROW GRAPHICS

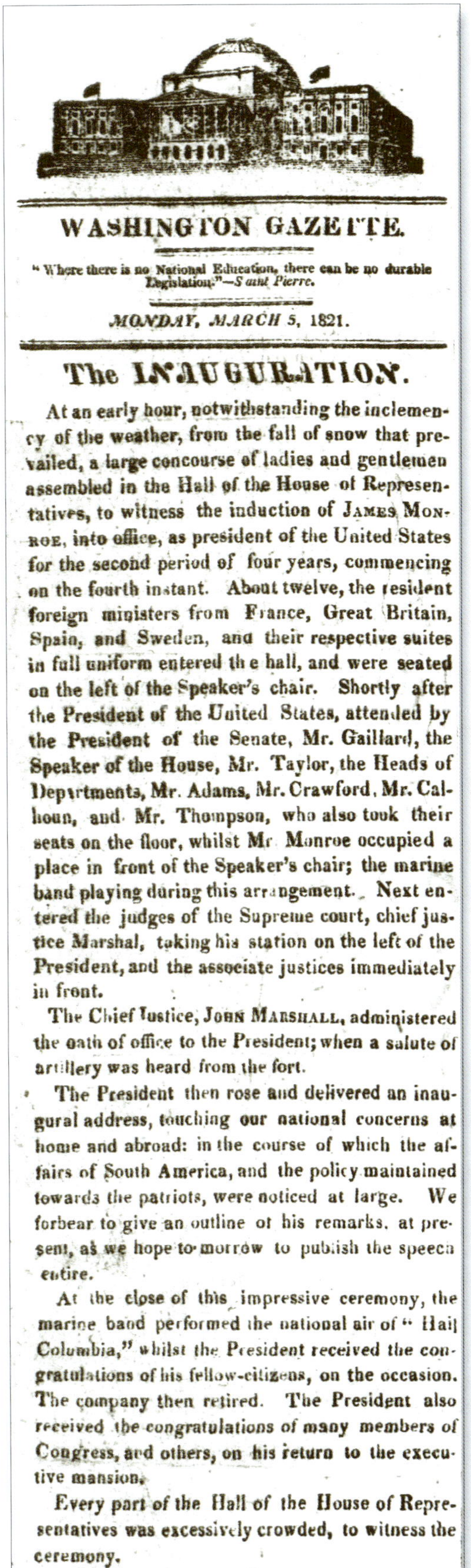

WASHINGTON GAZETTE.

"Where there is no National Education, there can be no durable Legislation."—Saint Pierre.

MONDAY, MARCH 5, 1821.

The INAUGURATION.

At an early hour, notwithstanding the inclemency of the weather, from the fall of snow that prevailed, a large concourse of ladies and gentlemen assembled in the Hall of the House of Representatives, to witness the induction of JAMES MONROE, into office, as president of the United States for the second period of four years, commencing on the fourth instant. About twelve, the resident foreign ministers from France, Great Britain, Spain, and Sweden, and their respective suites in full uniform entered the hall, and were seated on the left of the Speaker's chair. Shortly after the President of the United States, attended by the President of the Senate, Mr. Gaillard, the Speaker of the House, Mr. Taylor, the Heads of Departments, Mr. Adams, Mr. Crawford, Mr. Calhoun, and Mr. Thompson, who also took their seats on the floor, whilst Mr Monroe occupied a place in front of the Speaker's chair; the marine band playing during this arrangement. Next entered the judges of the Supreme court, chief justice Marshal, taking his station on the left of the President, and the associate justices immediately in front.

The Chief Justice, JOHN MARSHALL, administered the oath of office to the President; when a salute of artillery was heard from the fort.

The President then rose and delivered an inaugural address, touching our national concerns at home and abroad: in the course of which the affairs of South America, and the policy maintained towards the patriots, were noticed at large. We forbear to give an outline of his remarks, at present, as we hope to-morrow to publish the speech entire.

At the close of this impressive ceremony, the marine band performed the national air of "Hail Columbia," whilst the President received the congratulations of his fellow-citizens, on the occasion. The company then retired. The President also received the congratulations of many members of Congress, and others, on his return to the executive mansion.

Every part of the Hall of the House of Representatives was excessively crowded, to witness the ceremony.

James Monroe, by Samuel F. B. Morse. THE WHITE HOUSE

MORSE'S PORTRAIT

"I have been here nearly a fortnight; I commenced the President's portrait on Monday, and shall finish it tomorrow; I have succeeded to my satisfaction, and what is better to the satisfaction of himself & family, so much so that one of his daughters wishes me to copy the head for her; they all say that mine is the best that has been taken of him, the daughter told me, (she said in secret,) that her father was delighted with it and said it was the only one that in his opinion looked like him, and this too with Stuart's in the room."

—SAMUEL F. B. MORSE TO JEDIDIAH MORSE, 17 DECEMBER 1820

Newspaper account of Monroe's second inauguration.
CITY OF WASHINGTON GAZETTE, 21 MARCH 1821

SLAVERY

The controversy over slavery in the new state of Missouri alarmed nationalist leaders such as Monroe who saw it as a threat to the union. Monroe worked quietly behind the scenes in support of the compromise, urging congressmen to support it. He also wrote an anonymous essay for the Richmond newspaper, hoping to garner support for the compromise in Virginia (shown at right). Despite his concern Monroe, with his characteristic optimism, believed that the crisis would pass.

"I have never known a question so menacing to the tranquility and even the continuance of our Union as the present one. . . . As however there is a vast portion of intelligence & virtue in the body of the people, & the bond of Union has heretofore prov'd sufficiently strong to triumph over all attempts against it, I have great confidence that this effort will not be less unavailing."

Adapted by Arrow Graphics from a map in the University of Texas (Austin) Perry-Casteñeda Library Map Collection.

Monroe had long been an advocate of a plan of general emancipation in which all slaves would be freed and resettled somewhere outside the United States. The American Colonization Society established a colony for the relocation of free American blacks and named it Monrovia, in honor of President Monroe. Monrovia is today the capital of Liberia.

—Monroe to Thomas Jefferson, 19 February 1820

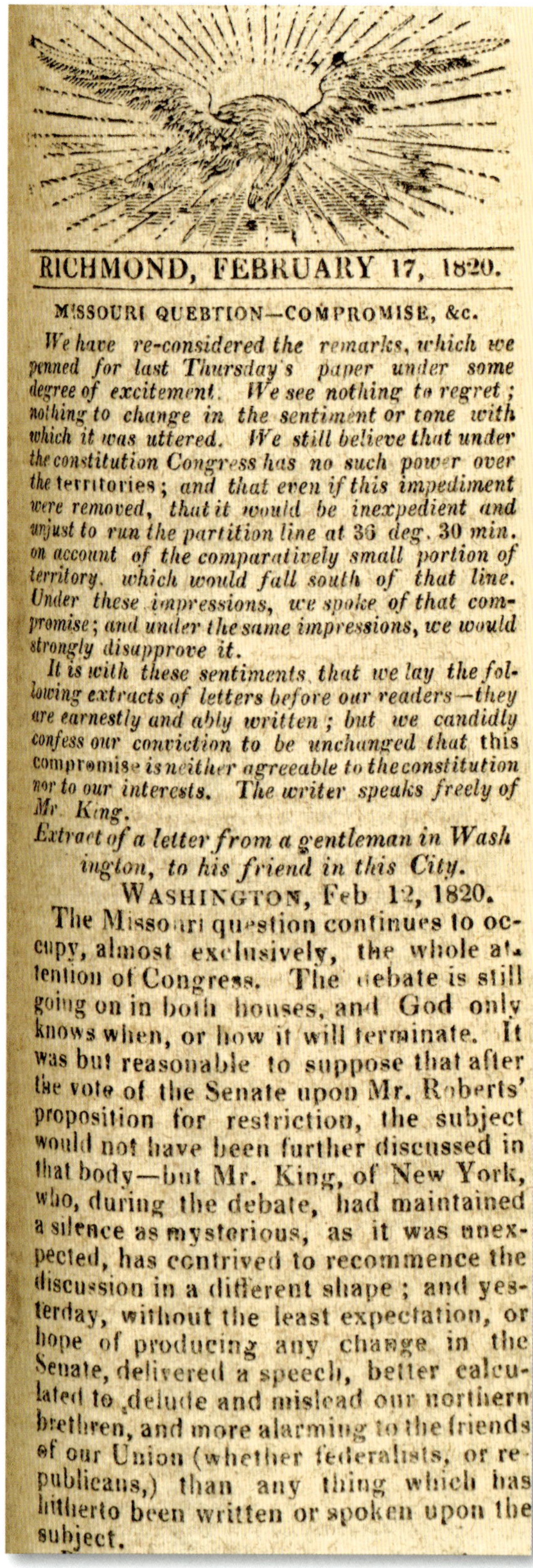

RICHMOND, FEBRUARY 17, 1820.

MISSOURI QUESTION—COMPROMISE, &c.

We have re-considered the remarks, which we penned for last Thursday's paper under some degree of excitement. We see nothing to regret; nothing to change in the sentiment or tone with which it was uttered. We still believe that under the constitution Congress has no such power over the territories; and that even if this impediment were removed, that it would be inexpedient and unjust to run the partition line at 36 deg. 30 min. on account of the comparatively small portion of territory, which would fall south of that line. Under these impressions, we spoke of that compromise; and under the same impressions, we would strongly disapprove it.

It is with these sentiments that we lay the following extracts of letters before our readers—they are earnestly and ably written; but we candidly confess our conviction to be unchanged that this compromise *is neither agreeable to the constitution nor to our interests. The writer speaks freely of Mr. King.*

Extract of a letter from a gentleman in Washington, to his friend in this City.

WASHINGTON, Feb 12, 1820.

The Missouri question continues to occupy, almost exclusively, the whole attention of Congress. The debate is still going on in both houses, and God only knows when, or how it will terminate. It was but reasonable to suppose that after the vote of the Senate upon Mr. Roberts' proposition for restriction, the subject would not have been further discussed in that body—but Mr. King, of New York, who, during the debate, had maintained a silence as mysterious, as it was unexpected, has contrived to recommence the discussion in a different shape; and yesterday, without the least expectation, or hope of producing any change in the Senate, delivered a speech, better calculated to delude and mislead our northern brethren, and more alarming to the friends of our Union (whether federalists, or republicans,) than any thing which has hitherto been written or spoken upon the subject.

Richmond Enquirer, 17 February 1820

A delegation of Indians from west of the Mississippi visited Washington in 1821. At the end of their visit they staged a ceremonial dance for President Monroe outside the White House. Baroness Hyde de Neuville, the wife of the French minister to the United States, painted the scene. COLONIAL WILLIAMSBURG FOUNDATION

Petalesharro, a Pawnee, was a member of the delegation to Washington. He is shown wearing a peace medal bearing the image of President Monroe.

PORTRAIT BY CHARLES BIRD KING, THE WHITE HOUSE

Presidents from Washington onward gave medals to Indians as symbols of peace and friendship. The Monroe peace medal was crafted by Moritz Furst in 1817.

JAMES MONROE MUSEUM

THE MONROE DOCTRINE

When Great Britain proposed in 1823 that the United States unite with it in a joint effort to prevent Spain and its allies from attacking the newly independent nations of Spanish America Monroe consulted with friends such as Jefferson and Madison and with his cabinet on the best course of action. After much deliberation Monroe decided to make a unilateral pronouncement condemning any effort by the European powers to reassert control over any independent nation in the Western Hemisphere (at right).

Monroe's pronouncement, now known as the Monroe Doctrine, was enunciated in his annual message to Congress of 2 December 1823. "We could not view any interposition for the purpose of oppressing [these new nations]," Monroe wrote, "or controlling in any other manner their destiny, by any European power in any other light than as the manifestation of an unfriendly disposition toward the United States."

Henry Clay, the powerful speaker of the House of Representatives, was a strong advocate of the independence movement in Spanish America, urging as early as 1817 that the United States extend diplomatic recognition to the revolutionary governments. President Monroe and Secretary of State Adams took a more cautious approach, delaying action until the new governments had demonstrated that they were functioning, independent entities. When the United States recognized the independence of Mexico and Gran Colombia in 1822 it was the first nation to do so.

PAINTING BY ALLYN COX IN THE U. S. CAPITOL

Henry Clay

PORTRAIT BY HENRY DARBY, U. S. SENATE

Maria Hester Monroe

BY CHARLES BIRD KING, ASH LAWN-HIGHLAND

Samuel Gouverneur

JAMES MONROE MUSEUM

Maria Hester Monroe, the Monroes' youngest daughter, married her cousin, Samuel Gouverneur of New York, in a ceremony at the White House on March 9, 1820. He was the son of Elizabeth Monroe's sister.

Lafayette's arrival at New York, 16 August 1824.

NEW YORK PUBLIC LIBRARY, EMMET COLLECTION

Marquis de Lafayette

In 1824 Congress, at Monroe's suggestion, invited the Marquis de Lafayette to visit the United States. He spent a year in the United States, traveling to all parts of the nation. He was greeted as a hero of the American Revolution, and the celebrations marking his visit were reminiscent of those honoring Monroe when he toured the nation. This portrait of Lafayette, painted by Samuel L. Waldo, once belonged to Monroe. COLONIAL WILLIAMSBURG FOUNDATION

John Quincy Adams

Andrew Jackson

THE 1824 ELECTION

Lafayette's visit to the United States coincided with the bitter presidential election of 1824. There were four candidates and, as a result, no one received a majority of the electoral vote. The election went to the House of Representatives, which had to decide between Andrew Jackson, who had the largest number of electoral votes, and John Quincy Adams, who placed second. The House elected Adams, and outraged Jackson supporters accused Adams of stealing the election. Monroe, not wishing to give the appearance of supporting any of the candidates, remained aloof from the election and even declined to attend social events hosted by any of the candidates.

Library of Congress, Prints and Photographs Division

Sculptor Felix DeWeldon created this statue of Monroe for a monument to him in Washington, D.C., that was never built. This smaller version is at the James Monroe Museum in Fredericksburg; another is at the State Department in Washington.

James Monroe Museum

THE LAST WORD

"I cannot conclude this communication, the last of the kind which I shall have to make, without recollecting with great sensibility and heartfelt gratitude the many instances of the public confidence and the generous support with which I have been honored. Having commenced my service in early youth, and continued it since with few and short intervals, I have witnessed the great difficulties to which our Union has been exposed, and admired the virtue and intelligence with which they have been surmounted. From the present prosperous and happy state I derive a gratification which I cannot express. That these blessings may be preserved and perpetuated will be the object of my fervent and unceasing prayers to the Supreme Ruler of the Universe."

Annual message to Congress, 7 December 1824

RETIREMENT

When James Monroe left the presidency in March 1825 he turned his attention to his personal finances. Monroe had incurred extensive debts during his years of public service when the salary he received was inadequate to cover the many expenses attendant to the office. In addition, his years of public service led to the neglect of his farms, and they had not been as productive as they could have been. Monroe successfully petitioned Congress for reimbursement of these expenses. He also sold Highland, his farm in Albemarle County. The revenue from these two sources allowed him to pay all his debts in 1828 and to spend the remainder of his life in fiscal solvency.

James Monroe, painted by Thomas Sully at Oak Hill in 1829.
U. S. Department of State, Washington, DC

Having sold Highland, the Monroes made Oak Hill their permanent home. Eliza and George Hay resided there with them and Maria and Samuel Gouverneur were frequent visitors (the Monroes also made a trip to New York in 1828 to visit them). Monroe, of course, remained involved in political affairs, but he now had more time for his family and his farm.

Monroe was a well educated man by the standards of his time. He had attended college, was well read, and could speak or read six languages. Even so, he always regretted that he had not had the time to pursue any intellectual or literary interests (although he had published a number of political essays and pamphlets). Retirement gave him the leisure to read and to write. During these last years Monroe wrote two book-length manuscripts—an autobiography and a study of political science entitled *The People the Sovereigns*. Both remained unpublished until well after Monroe died.

One activity that was of special interest to Monroe was the founding of the University of Virginia. Monroe, like many Virginians, had long espoused the creation of a state university. As early as 1792 he had written to Jefferson on the subject, asking "may we not hope as the country becomes exonerated from debt, publick & private, some considerable advance may be made for the establishment of [a state university]?" The assembly finally assented to the idea in 1816. Monroe, along with Jefferson and Madison, was appointed to the original board of visitors for the school, and in 1817 Monroe officiated at the laying of the cornerstone at the University of Virginia. He resigned as a visitor when he became president of the United States, but was reappointed in 1826 to fill the vacancy on the board created by the death of Thomas Jefferson. For the next several year Monroe and Madison (also a member of the board) devoted much of their time to the building of the university, which they saw as a monument to Jefferson's memory. Monroe served on the board until he resigned in 1831.

After his retirement from the presidency Monroe sold his farm in Albemarle County and made his home at Oak Hill in Loudoun County.
VIRGINIA HISTORICAL SOCIETY

Although Monroe had retired from public life he was repeatedly asked to assume some public office. Friends urged to run for governor and for vice-president; supporters of both Adams and Jackson asked him to be an elector for their candidate in the 1828 presidential election; and President Adams offered an appointment as a delegate to represent the United States at a pan-American conference in Panama in 1826. He declined all. He did, however, agree to fill two offices. He became a member of the Loudoun County court (the county's governing body), which was largely an honorary appointment for it entailed no actual duties, and he represented Loudoun County at a state-wide convention for the revision of Virginia's constitution in 1829. He served as president of the convention, but ill health forced him to resign from the convention before it finished its business.

The Monroes suffered from ill-health throughout the retirement years. Elizabeth Monroe's health had been poor since the days of their residence in London, and it declined greatly during the years following Monroe's retirement from the presidency. Monroe was a strong and vigorous man, but he too was plagued with chronic health problems, which were exacerbated by a fall from his horse in 1828. By the time of the constitutional convention both were in very bad health.

As is common with all older people, death began to take a regular toll among Monroe's friends and relations. His brother Joseph died in 1824 followed by his other brother, Andrew, in 1826, leaving James as the only surviving member of his family. The death in 1826 of Thomas Jefferson, who had been his friend since 1780, saddened him greatly. The greatest tragedy struck in September 1830. George Hay, who was also in poor health, had gone to the mineral springs in western Virginia for treatment. He died on September 21 while enroute back to Oak Hill. Two days later Elizabeth Monroe died after a lingering illness.

Monroe and Eliza Hay, devastated by these losses, decided to make an extended visit to Maria Gouverneur in New York. Monroe had intended to return to Virginia, but by spring 1831 he knew that this was not to be and that he would never return to his native state. He became bedridden and died on July 4, 1831.

Monroe was buried in an elaborate ceremony in New York City—an estimated 70,000 people, a larger assemblage of people than had ever gathered before in New York, witnessed his funeral procession. In 1858 the Virginia assembly decided to bring Monroe's body home. His remains were exhumed and taken to Richmond for burial in Hollywood Cemetery. The remains of Elizabeth Monroe and Maria Gouverneur, both of whom had been buried at Oak Hill (Eliza Hay is buried in Paris, where she died in 1840), were removed to the Monroe tomb in Richmond in 1903.

Virginia held a convention in 1829 to consider revisions to the state constitution. Monroe, a delegate from Loudoun County, served as president of the convention. This painting, by George Catlin, portrays Monroe seated in the governor's chair presiding over the proceedings. The figure addressing him is James Madison. Monroe suffered from ill health throughout the meeting and was forced to resign before the convention adjourned. VIRGINIA HISTORICAL SOCIETY

THE DEATH OF JEFFERSON

Thomas Jefferson, Monroe's mentor and long-time friend, died on July 4, 1826. Thomas Sully painted a full-length portrait of the elderly Jefferson (now owned by the U. S. Military Academy) and several portrait busts. The one shown here is displayed in the U. S. Senate. The copy that now hangs in the Rotunda of the University of Virginia was originally owned by Monroe.

"The late calamity with which you have been afflicted by the loss of your most estimable father, my friend, has given me the most heartfelt concern. Having been connected by the closest ties of friendship, with both your parents, from my earliest youth, I have always cherished the sentiments, with which I was animated at that period, with great interest, & have witnessed the late occurrence, with the deepest regret."

—Monroe to Martha Jefferson Randolph, 16 July 1826

"I thank you for your kindness in sending me a copy of your oration, on the death of Mr. Jefferson, which I have read with great interest & satisfaction. . . . Having studied the law under him in my youth, and been long engaged in the same career of public service since, I have known his great integrity, patriotism & important services. It is very gratifying to me to see a just tribute of respect paid to his memory.

—Monroe to John Tyler, 13 August 1826

Thomas Jefferson

Silhouette of James Monroe made during his retirement.
Jarvis S. Hanks, Metropolitan Museum of Art

James Monroe

Monroe, like Jefferson, Madison, and other leading Virginians, had long advocated the creation of a state university. The Virginia assembly finally authorized the building of a university in 1816. Monroe officiated at the laying of the cornerstone the following year. He was appointed to fill the vacancy on the board of visitors created by the death of Thomas Jefferson and served until his resignation in 1831.

Library of Congress, Prints and Photographs Division

Masonic apron worn by Monroe at the laying of the cornerstone for the University of Virginia. James Monroe Museum

Silhouettes of Eliza Monroe Hay, at left, and her daughter Hortensia. James Monroe Museum

Above and below: *Two sets of silhouettes of James and Elizabeth Monroe by Charles Willson Peale. The top set was probably made in Philadelphia in the early 1790s when Monroe was in the Senate. The lower pair was cut while Monroe was president.*

James Monroe Museum

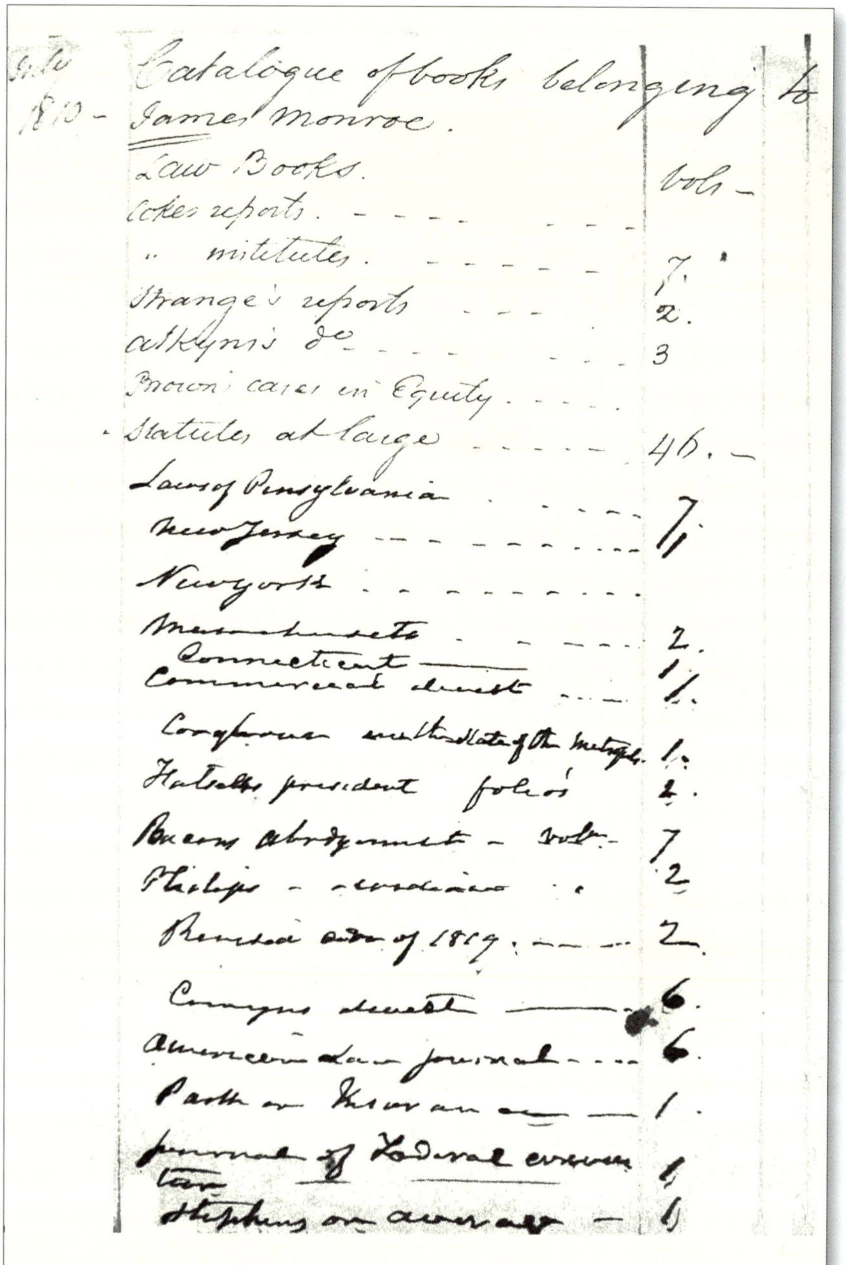

Catalogue of books belonging to James Monroe.

Law Books. vols

Cokes reports

" institutes. 7.

Strange's reports 2.

Atkyns's do 3

Brown's cases in Equity

Statutes at large 46.

Laws of Pensylvania

New Jersey 7

New york

Massachusetts 2.

Connecticut

American Law Journal 6.

Over his long career Monroe amassed an impressive collection of books that pertained primarily to government, law, and history. The James Monroe Museum has eighty books owned by Monroe and has collected approximately 100 titles owned by him. Monroe started making a list in 1810 of books he owned.

JAMES MONROE MUSEUM

James Monroe's bookplate

JAMES MONROE MUSEUM

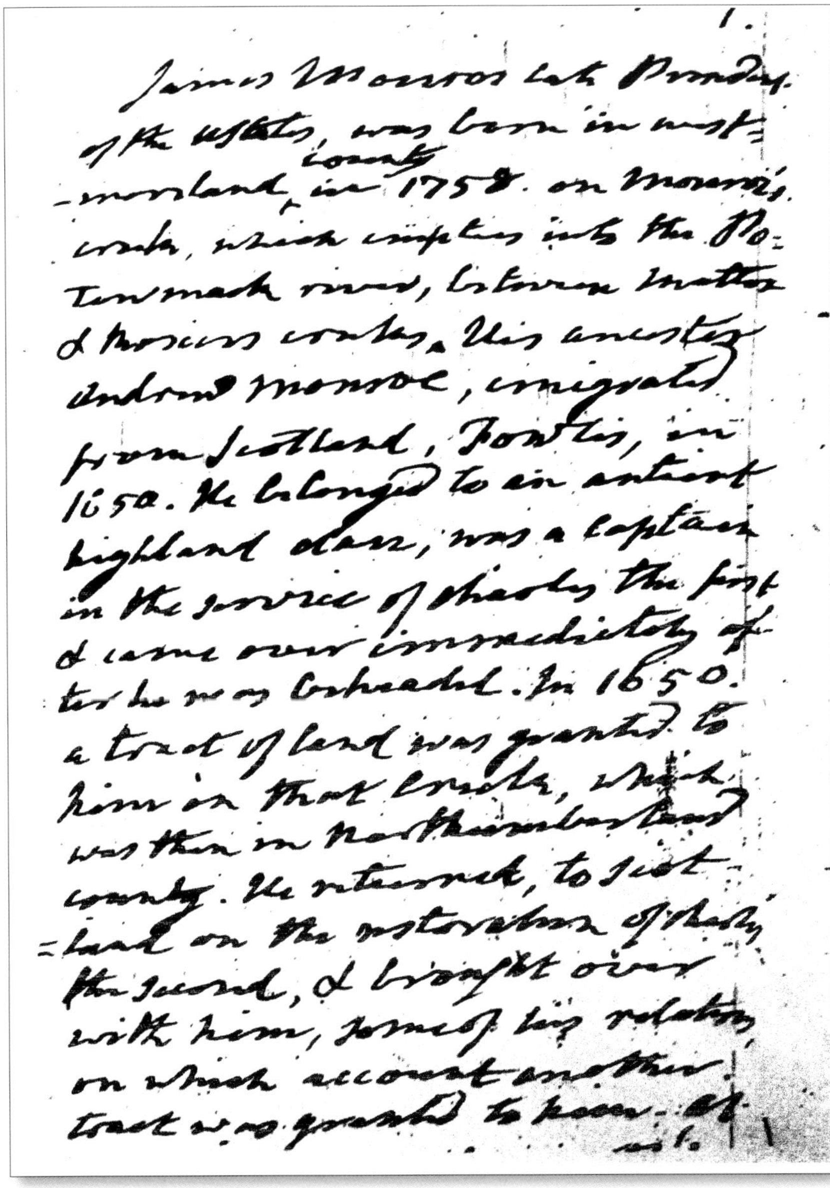

1.

James Monroe late Presidt.
of the U States, was born in West-
-moreland county, in 1758. on Monroe's
creek, which empties into the Po-
towmack river, between Mattox
& Popes creeks. His ancestor
Andrew Monroe, emigrated
from Scotland, Fowlis, in
1650. He belonged to an antient
highland clan, was a captain
in the service of Charles the first
& came over immediately af-
ter he was beheaded. In 1650.
a tract of land was granted to
him in that creek, which
was then in Northumberland
county. He returned, to Scot-
-land on the restoration of Charles
the second, & brought over
with him, some of his relations,
on which account another
tract was granted to him.

First page of Monroe's draft of his autobiography.

New York Public Library, Manuscript Division, Monroe Papers

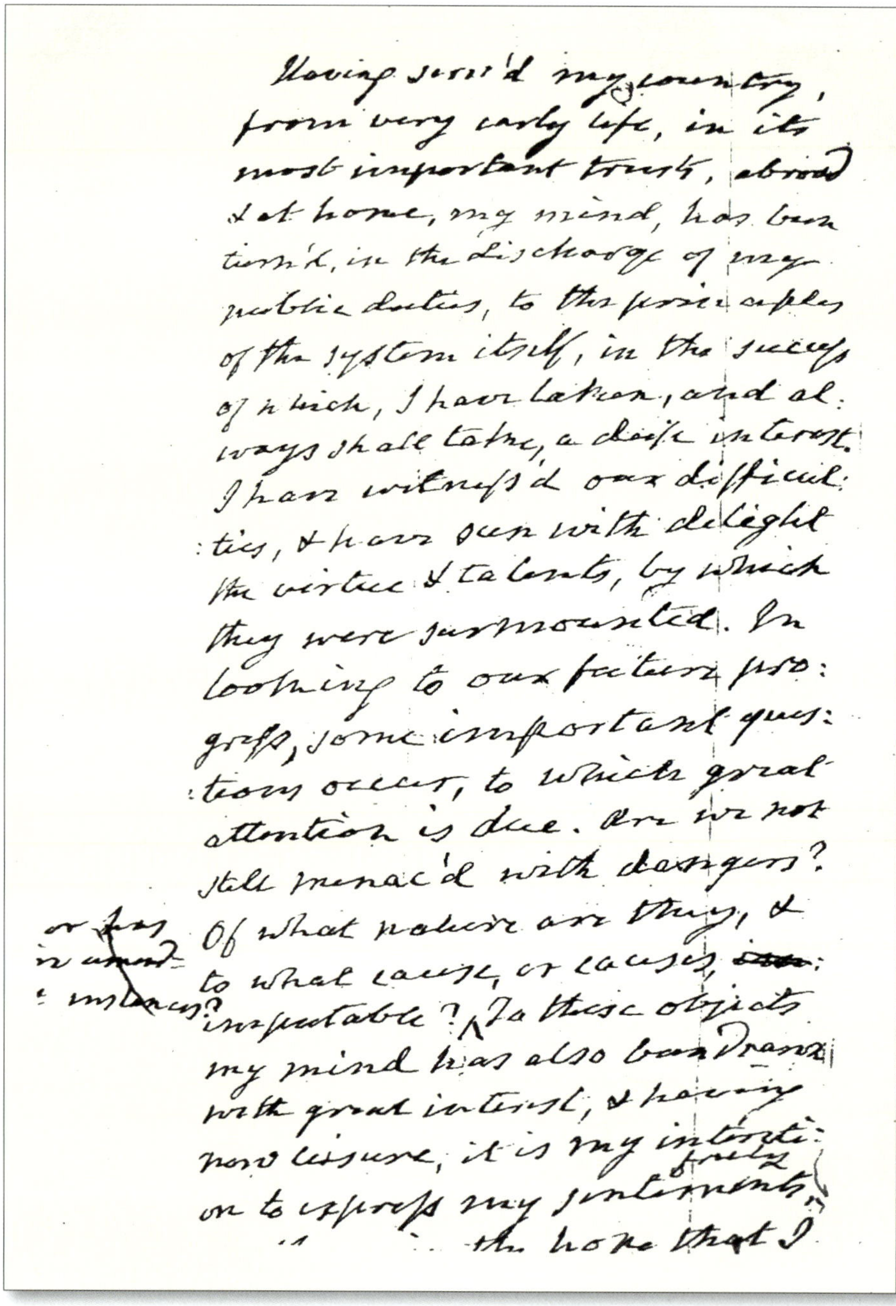

Having serv'd my country,
from very early life, in its
most important trusts, abroad
& at home, my mind, has been
turn'd, in the discharge of my
public duties, to the principles
of the system itself, in the success
of which, I have taken, and al:
ways shall take, a deep interest.
I have witness'd our difficul:
:ties, & have seen with delight
the virtue & talents, by which
they were surmounted. In
looking to our future pro:
gress, some important ques:
:tions occur, to which great
attention is due. Are we not
still menac'd with dangers?
Of what nature are they, &
to what cause, or causes,
imputable? To these objects
my mind has also been drawn
with great interest, & having
now leisure, it is my intenti:
on to express my sentiments, freely
the hope that I

First page of Monroe's draft of "The People the Sovereigns."

New York Public Library, Manuscript Division, Monroe Papers

DEATHS IN THE FAMILY

"We have both suffer'd, the most afflicting calamity that can befall us in this life, and which, if time may alleviate, it cannot efface. After having lived with the partner of your cares, in so many vicissitudes of life, so long together, and afforded to each other comforts, which no other person on earth can so do, as both of us have done, to have her snatched from us, is an affliction, which none but those who feel it, can justly estimate." —MONROE TO JAMES BROWN, 9 DECEMBER 1830

The Monroe family suffered a double tragedy in September 1830. George Hay, Monroe's son-in-law, died on September 21, and Elizabeth Monroe died two days later.

DIED]—on Friday last, at Mrs. Clark's, about eight miles from Charlottesville, on his return from the Virginia Springs, and after a long and lingering indisposition, GEORGE HAY, Esq., a Judge of the Federal Court, for the District of Virginia, and Son-in-law of Ex-President Monroe.—Mr. Hay was known to the United States, as well by the character he had won at the bar, as in the Republic of Letters.

RICHMOND ENQUIRER, 24 SEPTEMBER 1830

A letter received in Washington yesterday, announces the lamented decease, on Thursday last, at the family residence in Loudoun county, Virginia, of Mrs. MONROE, the respected consort of Ex-President MONROE.

BALTIMORE PATRIOT, 27 SEPTEMBER 1830

Monroe's final residence was the home of his daughter, Maria Gouverneur, on Prince Street in New York City. Ash Lawn-Highland

In 1831 the chair makers' guild of New York City honored Monroe by presenting him with a custom-made rocking chair. The chair, owned by the James Monroe Museum, is on display at Ash Lawn-Highland.

James Madison, painted by Joseph Wood

VIRGINIA HISTORICAL SOCIETY

"My ill state of health continuing . . . renders the restoration of my health very uncertain or indeed any favorable change in it. . . . I deeply regret that there is no prospect of our ever meeting again, since so long have we been connected . . . that a final separation is among the most distressing incidents which could occur."

—MONROE TO JAMES MADISON, 11 APRIL 1831

WASHINGTON.

THURSDAY, JULY 7, 1831.

The venerable Ex-President JAMES MONROE *closed his earthly career on the Anniversary of his Country's Independence.*

He breathed his last in the city of New York on Monday last, at half past three o'clock, the hand of death having been visibly upon him from eleven o'clock the preceding night. His bed-side was, during this long hovering of his wearied spirit on the confines of life and immortality, surrounded by his friends and physicians, whose attention and kindness have been unremitting during his illness. His death was easy, though so lingering, and to the last moment he retained his senses.

The circumstance of the death of this venerated patriot and statesman on the National Anniversary is not as extraordinary as the coincidence of the preceding deaths of two Ex-Presidents on the same day; but we think, if it had not been preceded by that most extraordinary concurrence of events, it would have been considered something beyond the common course of nature that, out of five living Ex-Presidents of the United States, three should have expired on the anniversary of the Declaration of that Independence which two of them, by their civil courage and wise counsels, and the third by his gallantry in the field, assisted in achieving.

We do not know what influence these occurrences may have on the minds of others, but to us they seem to add sanctity to the day of independence, and confirmation to the principles approved by its celebration. It is hardly possible that the anniversary can ever again arrive without our associating with it grateful and affecting recollections of the personal worth and public services of the patriots ADAMS, JEFFERSON, and MONROE.

Col. MONROE was, we believe, in his 73d year. His has been an eventful and busy life, almost entirely employed in public service. In the field, whilst a mere youth, he shed his blood for his country; and, with a no less zealous devotion to its interests, his best talents have ever since been exerted to promote them in the important stations of Member of Congress, Minister successively to France, Spain, and Great Britain, for seven years Secretary of State, Secretary of War, (during the trying six months preceding the last peace) and lastly, for eight years, as President of the United States. In all these stations he sustained the reputation of purity and uprightness, and maintained his country's rights with firmness, dignity, and ability; and he had the honor to retire from public life, after fifty years spent in the public service, poorer than he entered it. The evening of his life has been chequered with worldly troubles; but we have the satisfaction to know that its sun-set was serene and cloudless.

WASHINGTON NATIONAL INTELLIGENCER, *7 July 1831*

FUNERAL OF JAMES MONROE.

NEW YORK, July 8.

The funeral obsequies of the Ex-President JAMES MONROE were magnificent and impressive; not so much from any military array—though that was imposing—or costly escutcheons, as from the participation in them of a whole People. Not less than 70,000 persons witnessed the solemn spectacle! The line of march, which extended nearly two miles, was marked out by two dense rows of people, who, without guards or orders from any quarter, maintained their positions, and never once encroached upon the procession! The stoops, windows, and housetops, were alive with spectators. The decorum which prevailed amid this great throng was alike striking and creditable.

The following gentlemen were the officers of the day:

Grand Marshal—Major General Fleming,
Aids Brig.-General Doughty,
Brig.-General J. J. Jones,
Colonel Low,
Major Schermerhorn,
Capt. Tompkins,
Samuel Swartwout, Esq.
Silas E. Burrows, Esq.

The greatest credit is due to them and to the Committee of Arrangement of the Common Council, of which Alderman Cebra was Chairman, for the punctuality, order, and precision of the whole proceedings.

The body having been brought up by a Guard of Honor from the late residence of the deceased, accompanied by the immediate relatives and friends, was deposited on the platform in front of the City Hall. Immediately above it, a temporary stage, covered with black cloth, had been erected; and from that, President Duer, of Columbia College, made the following brief and appropriate remarks:

FELLOW CITIZENS.—Another anniversary of our national independence has been consecrated by the death of another of those patriots who assisted to achieve it—of another of those statesmen, who, after a long course of public service, attained the highest office in that Government, to the foundation of which he had contributed by an early devotion of life and fortune to his country.

Did this event stand single in our annals—were it unconnected in our memories with the deaths on a former anniversary of the same glorious day—of two of his illustrious predecessors—even then a similar removal of the deceased would have been deemed admonitory, and would have commanded a solemn and appropriate notice. But following as it does that signal union in their flight from this world of the immortal spirits of Adams and Jefferson, the departure of Monroe must impress us

WASHINGTON NATIONAL INTELLIGENCER, *11 July 1831*

LYING IN STATE AT THE CITY HALL, NEW YORK

In 1858 the Virginia assembly voted to make arrangements for the return of Monroe's body to his native state. After the exhumation, the body lay in state at New York's city hall. The remains were then placed on a steamboat and taken to Richmond where they were re-interred at Hollywood Cemetery on July 5, 1858 in an elaborate ceremony. Harper's Weekly of July 1858 carried four illustrations of the ceremonies in New York and Richmond.

THE LANDING AT RICHMOND

EXUMING THE REMAINS OF PRESIDENT MONROE IN THE SECOND STREET CEMETERY

THE CEREMONY AT THE GRAVE, IN HOLLYWOOD CEMETERY, RICHMOND

Death mask of James Monroe

Fenimore Art Museum, Cooperstown, NY

The Monroe tomb in Hollywood Cemetery in Richmond. The bodies of Elizabeth Monroe and Maria Monroe Gouverneur were re-interred here in 1903.

Library of Congress, Prints and Photographs Division

James Monroe

painted by Thomas Sully at Oak Hill in 1829.
United States Military Academy, West Point, NY